THE SURFACE OF
THE EARTH

T0381585

THE SURFACE OF THE EARTH

ELEMENTARY
PHYSICAL AND ECONOMIC GEOGRAPHY

BY

HERBERT PICKLES, B.A., B.Sc.

(*Revised by* ELLIS W. HEATON *formerly Headmaster
of Tynemouth Municipal High School*)

Cambridge :

at the University Press

1937

CAMBRIDGE
UNIVERSITY PRESS

University Printing House, Cambridge CB2 8BS, United Kingdom

Published in the United States of America by Cambridge University Press, New York

Cambridge University Press is part of the University of Cambridge.

It furthers the University's mission by disseminating knowledge in the pursuit of
education, learning and research at the highest international levels of excellence.

www.cambridge.org
Information on this title: www.cambridge.org/9781107651524

First edition 1915
Reprinted 1918, 1920, 1921
Second edition 1925
Third edition 1927
Fourth edition 1937
First published 1937
First paperback edition 2014

A catalogue record for this publication is available from the British Library

ISBN 978-1-107-65152-4 Paperback

PREFACE TO THE SECOND EDITION

THE purpose of this book is to provide a readable account of the earth's surface and the changes that are taking place upon it, and to show how human activities are influenced by physical and climatic factors.

The course set forth is intended as an introduction to a formal study of the world, for children of about ten to twelve years of age, and an attempt has been made to present the matter in such a way as to foster a love for the subject.

The first eleven chapters deal with land-forms, the action of natural forces, climate and the great natural regions, each considered in relation to man's life and work. The remaining chapters are devoted chiefly to human activities—especially to the way in which the world's products are handled and used by man. Progress with respect to transport is recorded—up to 1923.

Chief amongst the new matter in the second edition is Chapter XII, which marks stages in the development of agricultural communities and the decline of nomadism. Whilst making the survey of the surface of the earth more nearly complete, this chapter will serve, it is hoped, as a link between geography and simple lessons on world history.

It may be added that the book covers the syllabus of the "Second Stage" outlined in the *Suggestions for the Teaching of Geography* (Circular 834) issued by the Board of Education.

Amongst the Exercises will be found many devised for the purpose of encouraging map-study; they should be of service in training pupils to undertake independent work.

Great pains have been taken to provide adequate photographic illustration. Some photographs have been taken for the specific purpose of illustrating this volume; but the following have generously provided prints, and the author wishes to express his appreciation of their assistance:

The High Commissioner for New Zealand, The Geological Department of the University of Leeds, The North Eastern Railway Company, The Port of London Authority, The Canadian National Railways, The Malay States Information Agency, The Ullswater Navigation and Transit Company, The *Daily Sketch*, Messrs Lever Brothers Limited, The Cunard Co., The Aire and Calder Navigation, Mr Godfrey Bingley, Dr W. H. Barber, Mr G. W. Collinson, Mr W. H. Greenwood, B.A., Mr F. Haworth, M.Sc., and Mr H. G. Ponting, F.R.G.S.

H. P.

Leeds,
April, 1924.

PREFACE TO THE FOURTH EDITION

The statistical information in the latter part of the book has been brought up-to-date and a new paragraph on the Conquest of the Air has been written by Mr Ellis W. Heaton, formerly Headmaster of Tynemouth Municipal High School.

January, 1937.

CONTENTS

ILLUSTRATIONS

MAPS AND DIAGRAMS

The illustrations on pages 14, 17, 27, 34, 39, 46, 47, 53, 91 are from copyright photographs taken by Mr Godfrey Bingley, and lent by the Geological Department of the University of Leeds. Copyright photographs were also lent by Dr W. H. Barber (page 11), Mr W. H. Greenwood, B.A. (pages 4, 60, 62), Mr F. Haworth, M.Sc. (pages 61, 63), Mr H. G. Ponting, F.R.G.S. (page 133) and Mr G. W. Collinson (page 25). The photographs on pages 21, 28, 30, 55, 88, 90, 92, 99, 132, 134, 159, 165, 167, 171 are reproduced by courtesy of the North Eastern Railway Co.; those on pages 74, 126, 130, 149, 174 by courtesy of the Canadian National Railways; those on pages 59, 125, 127 by courtesy of the High Commissioner for New Zealand; those on pages 19, 162, 163 by courtesy of the Port of London Authority; those on pages 42, 120 by courtesy of the Malay States Information Agency; those on pages 51, 100, 107 (Messrs Abraham and Son's Series) by courtesy of the Ullswater Navigation and Transit Co.; those on pages 3, 117 and 156 by courtesy of the *Daily Sketch*, Lever Brothers Limited, and the Cunard Co. respectively, and those on pages 164, 168, 170 by courtesy of the Aire and Calder Navigation.

I. RAIN

On a warm day after a heavy shower of rain, you will have noticed that the surface of the road quickly becomes dry. What becomes of the water ? Some of it is carried away by drains, but perhaps you have sometimes seen the road **steaming** and discovered that part of the moisture passes into the air, in the form of water-vapour.

When wet clothes are hung in the open air, or placed before a fire, they lose their moisture in the same manner. Wherever a sheet of water is exposed to the air, the same process, called **evaporation,** is constantly in progress. Think what a great quantity of vapour must daily pass into the atmosphere from the surface of great oceans thousands of miles in extent.

We must now consider what becomes of the moisture which the atmosphere has gained. You have seen clouds floating across the sky, sometimes white and beautiful when they reflect the sunlight, but often, and especially in wet weather, black and heavy-looking.

Sometimes clouds are to be seen hanging about the summits of hills and mountains, and if you were to ascend a hill thus capped with cloud your clothing would become damp or even wet.

From the summit of a mountain, clouds may sometimes be seen floating at a lower level. The photograph on the opposite page was taken during the Balkan war from a warplane when above a bank of clouds.

The river shown is the Maritza. On its banks is the city of Adrianople, concealed from view by the clouds.

Rain-clouds—breaking up.

When a cloud is very near the surface of the earth we call it **fog.**

You will have guessed by now that clouds are composed of tiny drops of water, derived from the moisture which is always passing into the atmosphere by the process of evaporation. The change has been produced by cold. Water-vapour is an invisible

Above the Clouds. A photograph taken from a warplane.

gas, but when cooled it changes into a mass of tiny
drops of water. Fill a tumbler with cold water and
place it in a warm room. Though you cannot see any
moisture in the atmosphere of the room, the outer
surface of the tumbler soon becomes *clouded*, and
you may even see drops of water trickle down its sides.

Clouds are carried along by winds over the land,
and are caused by mountains to pass upwards to cooler

Clouds forming about the summit of a mountain. (Dent Blanche.)

levels in the atmosphere, where further **condensation**
takes place, and rain falls upon the earth.

You will therefore expect that mountainous districts
receive more rain than flat areas.

If you examine a rainfall map of the British Isles
you will find this to be true. The wettest place in
England is Seathwaite, a village situated amongst
the mountains of the Lake District.

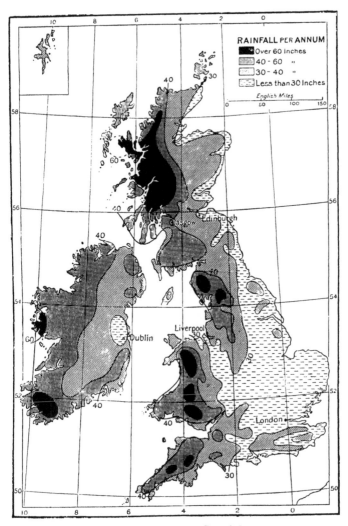

Fig. 1. Rainfall map. British Isles.

You will notice that the western side of Britain—the more mountainous part of the country—is much wetter than the eastern. Our rain-bearing winds come from the west and south-west—from the Atlantic Ocean, and lose a great deal of their moisture during their journey over the high land.

In order to make a rainfall map, it is necessary to measure the amount of rain which falls day by day. Take a dish with vertical sides, and place it outside on a wet day. If you find the water collected by it is half an inch deep, you say that the rainfall for that day is **half an inch.**

But collecting rainwater in a dish would not be an accurate way of measuring rainfall. Some would be lost, for you know that evaporation is always taking place ; besides loss might occur by splashing. So a vessel specially constructed to prevent loss is used. It is called a **rain-gauge,** and its parts are shown in Fig. 2.

The vessel *A* carries a funnel which collects rain and passes it into vessel *B*. Then by means of a measuring-glass, the rainfall on the area equal to the top of the gauge can be found.

Many hundreds of these rain-gauges are in use in the British Isles. They are examined every day, and a record of the rainfall throughout the year is made.

The records are sent to a central office in London, and used in map-making.

Snow is of course collected by the gauge, and when melted is registered as rain.

It has been found that at the summit of Ben Nevis, the highest mountain in the British Isles, the rainfall is over 200 inches per annum ; at Fort William, near the foot of the mountain, it is about 100 inches ; whilst on the east coast of England, the annual fall is only 20 inches.

At Seathwaite (mentioned above) the yearly rainfall is well over 100 inches, the average for a number of years being 130.

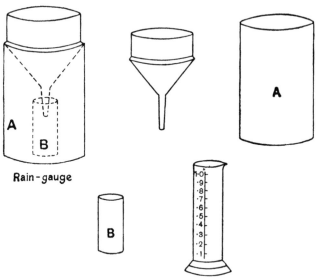

Rain-gauge

Fig. 2. Rain-gauge and its parts.

The measuring-glass is drawn on a large scale to show the graduations clearly. It will hold a quantity of water which, spread over an area equal to the top of the gauge, would be one inch deep.

Rain is necessary for plant-life. Where it does not fall in sufficient quantity, agriculture can only be carried on by means of irrigation ; i.e. drawing water from rivers along channels cut through the cultivated tracts. This is done in Spain, Italy, Egypt and many other countries.

The richest vegetation in the world is found in the basins of the Amazon and the Congo, where the climate is hot, and rainfall is very heavy. Regions where rainfall is very slight are desert. There is hardly any vegetation, and therefore no animal life. The Sahara in North Africa, and the central part of Australia are great tracts of this kind.

India, unlike England, has two well-marked seasons. A hot wet season begins in April, and extends to October. During these months, rain-bearing wind blows from the Indian Ocean over the land. It is called **the Monsoon.**

From October to April the climate is cooler and dry. The wind blows from the land to the ocean.

When rain falls upon the earth then, some, which fails to sink into the ground, passes back into the atmosphere. Another portion helps to support plant-life.

The rest may flow over the surface of the land as rivers, or sink into the earth. What happens to these two portions we shall consider in the next chapter.

EXERCISES

1. Make a diagram to show (roughly) the height of the land along a line from St David's Head to Harwich. Write on the diagram the rainfall in inches at a number of places, and so show its relation to altitude and distance from the west coast.

2. On an outline map of England shade areas which would have heavy rainfall if moisture-bearing winds came from the east.

3. Using a rainfall map of the world, make a list of regions which have heavy rainfall, and a second list of places where rainfall is very slight.

II. RIVERS AND THEIR WORK

When rain falls upon the earth, some of it sinks into the ground and makes its way deeper and deeper, until its downward course is stopped by something, such as a bed of clay, through which water cannot pass.

Fig. 3. Section of Hill, to show origin of Spring at *S*. *a* and *b* are porous beds; they store water which is prevented from sinking lower by the impervious bed *c*.

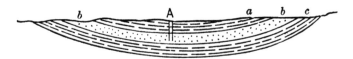

Fig. 4. Artesian Well.

a and *c* are impervious, *b* is porous. No spring will be formed, owing to the basin-like arrangement of the beds; but the water stored may be reached by sinking a shaft at *A*.

The water then finds its way along the surface of the clay, and in course of time probably reaches daylight again at a lower level. There it comes bubbling out of the ground, and we say there is a **spring**. Perhaps you have noticed a belt of moist or marshy land along a hill-side ; it marks the junction of porous beds, through which water passes, and impervious ones.

Very often spring water contains mineral matter which it has dissolved during its underground journey. Sometimes the water is even warm, especially in those areas where volcanoes have once existed.

Mineral waters are often of value because they assist in the cure of certain diseases. People go to

The mouth of Gaping Ghyll.
(Diameter, 15 to 20 feet.)

Harrogate in Yorkshire, to Marienbad and other places on the continent to "take the waters." The warm springs at Bath have been famous since the days of the Romans in Britain. But perhaps the most wonderful hot springs in the world are those of Yellowstone Park in North America. Many others are known in Iceland and in New Zealand.

Limestone in particular is soluble in water, and in limestone areas such as Derbyshire and West Yorkshire, the action of water on the rock has produced magnificent scenery. In such areas, deep and narrow

Climbing out of a Pot-hole, by means of a rope-ladder.

valleys called **gorges** are cut in the surface of the earth by streams ; whilst underground, solution of the rock results in the formation of great caverns. The latter frequently have a connection with the

surface by means of almost vertical shafts called
pot-holes, which are produced partly by solution and
partly by the grinding action of pebbles swept along
by the stream.

Into such natural shafts rivers plunge, continue
their course underground, and emerge lower down.

Malham Cove.

Many Yorkshire streams are of this type. A short
distance after leaving Malham Tarn, the Aire dis-
appears, travels underground for over a mile and
emerges at Malham Cove, at the foot of a limestone
cliff 300 feet high.

One of the most famous pot-holes in the Pennine
region is Gaping Ghyll. It is over 300 feet deep.

Sometimes the weight of the undermined rock causes the roof of a cavern to fall in. Afterwards the stream may be seen flowing at the bottom of a deep gorge whose sides are walls of limestone.

In America, gorges of tremendous depth have been carved out by some rivers. They occur especially in dry areas, where there is very little **side-wash** to wear away the banks, and the river continues to bore deeper and deeper. The Grand Cañon of the Colorado is in some places 6000 feet deep.

The water from a spring trickles down the hillside making for itself a little channel in the soil. Soon it is joined by other tiny streams called "tributaries." These have their **source** either in other springs, or in rainwater which did not sink into the earth.

Thus a river is formed which flows onward and ever downward, seeking lower ground. Fragments of rock which fall into the stream are smoothed and rounded by being rolled against each other, and the particles removed in the process, together with soil washed from the banks, and even pebbles, are carried along by the current. But you must see a mountain torrent, swollen by heavy rains, to discover what a river is really capable of doing. Huge boulders are rolled far from their former resting-places. Bridges are sometimes swept away, and deep overflow channels worn in the softer rocks.

Where does all the material transported by a river go ? You will be able to answer this question if you follow the stream. In making its way to lower ground, the path taken by a river will naturally be anything but straight. Now if you watch water

A gorge in limestone—Gordale Scar.

flowing round a bend, you will at once notice that the water on the inside flows more slowly than the rest. You can prove this by throwing pieces of wood or paper into the stream.

You will also find that the water which moves slowly is depositing sediment—the pebbles and earthy

A River-bend.

The excess of ice on the left-hand side indicates that there the water is flowing more slowly than on the right. Notice also that tree-roots have been exposed on one side, and sediment (covered with snow) has been deposited on the opposite bank.

matter which it has carried from above. New land is actually being built up by the stream.

When we examine the outside of the bend, however, we find that the ground is being worn away by the water which flows briskly against it. You may find that roots of trees have been uncovered, and so understand why trees sometimes fall across a stream. A river then is constantly engaged in making the bends in its course more pronounced.

If you examine the maps of England and Scotland, you will find that every river has a winding course ; and some, for example, the Thames, the Tees, and the Forth are extremely crooked.

Sometimes a stream flows into a lake. A very muddy river called the Rhone enters Lake Geneva. But the overflow from the opposite end of the lake, still named Rhone, is a beautiful clear river. The mud has been dropped on to the floor of the lake—a consequence of the almost stationary condition of the water.

All rivers, however, succeed in carrying sediment as far as the sea, and if there is not a strong tide, new land is built up about the mouth of the river.

Look at the Italian river Po, which flows into the Adriatic Sea ; the Nile, emptying itself into the Mediterranean ; and the Mississippi, pouring its muddy waters into the Gulf of Mexico.

In each case it is plain that new land has been formed, through which the river flows by several channels to the sea. The town of Adria which gave its name to the Adriatic Sea is now about twenty miles inland.

Often these patches of new land are triangular in shape, like a certain Greek letter, Δ, whose name, **delta,** is used to describe them.

It is easy to understand that the river which builds a delta is not a good commercial stream. Its best channel has to be selected and kept clear by constant dredging, if ships are to enter it.

High Cup Ghyll, near Appleby.

Notice the winding course of the river. The tributaries come mainly from the slope on the right, where a line of springs marks the junction of limestone and slate beds.

The Thames, you will notice, reaches the sea by one broad channel called an **estuary.** It is entered

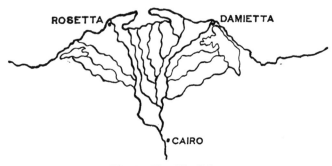

Fig. 5. The Nile Delta.

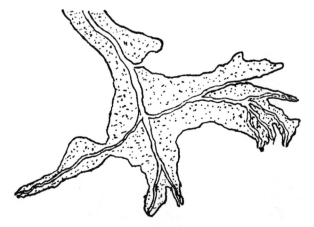

Fig. 6. The end of the Mississippi Delta. (After Chamberlin and Salisbury.)

by the tide twice a day, and that is a great help to shipping. Yet even in the Thames dredging is constantly being carried on to make a channel suitable for ocean-liners.

When river-water reaches the sea, sediment is dropped for two reasons : (i) the speed of the stream is checked, and (ii) the presence of salt favours the deposition of solid matter.

A Thames Dredger, Tilbury Dock.

It might be supposed that when the tide is **going out** sediment would be removed from the estuary. But it is not until the water is very low that the sandy bottom is disturbed ; and before the material can be carried far, the tide is coming in again, sometimes bringing sediment from other parts of the coast.

What frequently happens is that a **bar is built** near the entrance to the estuary.

In the Mersey sandbanks are very troublesome, and it has been found rather difficult to provide a good channel to suit the gigantic vessels of to-day.

It is proposed that walls shall be built, one on each side of the best channel—the Crosby Channel. These walls will stand above low-water level to the height of five feet, and it is expected that they will prevent the sand from being washed into Crosby Channel.

There is something else to notice about the course of a river.

It often happens that a bed of hard rock is found lying amongst the softer rocks. The latter are more easily worn away by water, so that a difference in level is established. Once this is done the work proceeds at a rapid rate, and soon the stream is tumbling from the high, hard ledge in a **waterfall,** on to the softer rocks below.

The hard ledge is usually undermined, and in course of time a large piece will break away, so that the waterfall is pushed a little further up-stream. Great waterfalls are not common in England. High Force in the river Tees is one of our best.

The greatest falls in the world are those at Niagara in America, and the Victoria Falls of the Zambesi in Africa. In each case there is a gorge several miles long below the falls. The gorge is constantly being lengthened, for the river is always wearing away the rock over which it rushes, and so, slowly but surely, pushing the waterfall further up-stream.

Waterfalls greatly reduce the value of a river as a means of communication. Canals are sometimes cut, as at Niagara, to enable vessels to avoid them.

On the other hand they form a valuable source of power for manufactures, because they can be made to set machinery in motion.

The St Anthony Falls, on the Mississippi, drive the machinery in the flour-mills of Minneapolis.

The great power of Niagara is used to produce electricity, which is carried by cable to distant industrial towns, where it is utilised in workshops and factories.

High Force.

The waterfall is due to the occurrence, amidst limestone strata, of a bed of hard igneous rock.

In countries where rainfall is slight, rivers are of great value for watering the land. Egypt is sometimes called the "Gift of the Nile," for the country has always been dependent on the Nile floods for irrigation of the land, and the soil itself is river-silt.

In 1902 a great dam was completed across the river near Assuan, to regulate the flow of water into the irrigation canals, and agriculture can now be carried on under excellent conditions. The river Tigris is now being treated in the same way, for the purpose of irrigating the land of Mesopotamia, which is expected to become an important wheat-growing region.

Rivers form the natural means of entering a country. An interesting illustration of this is found in the history of England. When our forefathers crossed the North Sea, seeking a new home, they entered Britain by such estuaries as the Thames, Orwell, Wash, Humber, and established settlements on their banks.

At a much later date Europeans began to emigrate to America ; and the early colonies were founded on the banks of rivers—the Hudson, Delaware and St Lawrence.

The fertility of the alluvial soil in valleys, and the advantage offered by rivers for irrigation, also attract population.

The valleys of some of the great rivers of Asia and Africa are the most densely populated areas in the world. The basins of the Hwangho, named **China's Sorrow** because of the destruction which follows the bursting of its banks, the Yangtse, the Si-kiang, are occupied by millions of people. The valleys of the Ganges, of the Indus and of the African Nile have been densely populated for ages.

On the other hand when you examine the map of northern Asia, you notice great rivers, the Ob-Irtish, the Yenesei and the Lena, which flow from the huge central mountain systems, across the Siberian plain to the Arctic Ocean. Though the soil of northern Asia is not poor, the region has a very small population because the climatic conditions are so unfavourable. The ground is frozen hard during the long dreary winter. The rivers become free from ice in the upper parts first, with the result that floods often cover miles of land lower down.

There are, however, many towns on the upper reaches of the rivers, and population is steadily increasing.

Another reason that leads people to settle on the banks of rivers is the value of streams as a means of communication. Some of the European rivers, the Rhine, Danube and Volga, which flow for a great distance through almost level country are particularly important as waterways. You will notice that population is often concentrated:

(1) Where two rivers join: e.g., Lyons (Rhone-Saône); Coblenz (Rhine-Moselle), a fortress-town commanding the Moselle Valley; St Louis (Mississippi-Missouri).

(2) Where an important route crosses a river, e.g., York (on the Ouse) and Perth (on the Tay), both founded long ago on the great road from south to north, and because of their position, now important railway junctions.

(3) At the highest point that can be reached by sea-going vessels, e.g., London and Bristol.

EXERCISES

1. Make a map to show the course you think the head-waters of the Thames would follow if the gap between the Chilterns and the White Horse Downs were blocked up

2. Upon what does the swiftness of a stream depend ? Arrange in order of swiftness the rivers Great Ouse, Spey, Wye, giving reasons for your arrangement.

3. Invent a map to show a river receiving tributaries on each bank, forming a lake in its course, and entering the sea by an estuary. Mark three points, *A, B, C*, where towns would be likely to arise.

4. Find on your maps of England, Scotland, and Ireland, six "confluence-towns" (i.e. towns situated where rivers join). Make a diagram showing the situation in each case.

5. Name important confluence-towns in America, Asia and Africa, and give the names of the rivers.

6. Make diagrams to show that the following river-valleys have been utilised in railway construction : Tyne ; Tay and Spey ; Morava and Maritza (Balkan Peninsula).

N.B. Collect picture post-cards showing river-valleys, gorges, waterfalls, etc., and keep them in an album.

III. SEDIMENTARY ROCKS

We have noticed already that rivers are builders of new land. They are ceaselessly engaged in destroying and building up. The product of their destructive action in one place is used in the formation of new land elsewhere.

They deposit sediment on the floor of the sea, on the bottom of lakes, on their own beds, and on the land they overflow in times of flood.

Leaves and branches of trees which fall into the water float away with the stream, but in course of time become water-logged and sink.

The remains of creatures which once lived on the land or in the water also drop to the bottom. All these relics are buried in the sand or mud.

As the layer of sediment increases in thickness it becomes compressed, so that the surface in the central part is made almost parallel to the base. Probably some mineral solution finds its way into the mass, and, cementing the particles together, forms hard solid rock. If it were possible for such a mass to be raised above the water, what would it look like ?

Fossiliferous Limestone.

We find an answer to this question when we visit a quarry where sandstone or limestone is being worked.

We notice two things in the quarry. First, the rocks are arranged in parallel beds—though not always in a horizontal position. Secondly, **fossils,** that is, models of plants or animals in lime or some other mineral substance, are to be found in the rocks. These two discoveries at once remind us of the work done by a river.

The material carried by a river is spread out in parallel beds, and it is easy to understand that as the body of an animal buried in sediment gradually decomposes, it will be replaced by mineral matter, i.e. become fossilised. We therefore conclude that the rocks we are examining are the result of work done by water in past ages. Because of their mode of origin, such rocks are named "sedimentary." The surface rocks over the greater part of England are of this type, and it follows that the land in which we live was once below the level of the sea. The fact of the matter is, that not England only, but all other lands have been submerged, wholly or partly, several times in the course of their history.

Perhaps at first it is difficult to believe this. But sea-shells are very common in sedimentary rocks, and their presence cannot be satisfactorily explained in any other way.

It will be interesting to consider the subject a little further.

There is proof that land has been submerged in comparatively recent times at many places round our coasts. In the Wirral peninsula in Cheshire for example, there is a **submerged forest,** which consists of the remains of vegetation that must have flourished, formerly, well above high-water mark. It is now being gradually swept away by the sea, and will soon have disappeared entirely.

Again, you will notice a great number of inlets on the west coast of Scotland, the south-west of Ireland and the coast of Norway. Many of these have been carefully examined and found to be **drowned valleys,** that is, valleys which have been flooded by the sea.

Some of them are submerged lake-basins; for the water is shallower at the entrance than further in the fjord.

Now, if you examine a physical map of England, you will notice a long curved and broken ridge of high land, which extends through the Marlborough Downs in Wiltshire, the Chiltern Hills, East Anglian Heights, Lincolnshire Wolds and Yorkshire Wolds, to the sea at Flamborough Head.

Submerged Forest on the Cheshire Coast.

There it terminates in magnificent white or grey cliffs, three to four hundred feet high, and peopled with thousands of sea-fowl.

It is called the **Chalk Ridge,** and is really the edge of the bed of chalk which extends far to the east under other layers of sediment; these, being on top of the chalk, must be of more recent formation.

When the chalk is carefully examined, and for this

The Northern end of the Chalk Ridge.   (Bempton.)
(An egg-gatherer on the edge of the cliff is about to descend.)

purpose a small portion must be powdered and placed under a microscope, it is found to be composed of the remains of tiny creatures which once lived in sea-water. We learn from this that the chalk bed was built up on the floor of the sea. Indeed similar creatures live at the present day in the surface waters of the Atlantic, and their remains are forming a deposit on the bed of the ocean.

The Cotswolds, the Northampton Heights, and the North York Moors are all parts of a **limestone ridge**. The rock is named Oolitic limestone, because its particles are small rounded grains like the roe of a fish (oolite = eggstone). The grains become round by being rolled about in water. The Pennines are also composed chiefly of limestone—the Carboniferous Limestone, so named because it forms part of that great series of sedimentary rocks wherein occur most of our coal-seams. This limestone again is exceedingly rich in the fossilised remains of marine creatures.

In addition to those already mentioned there are several other distinct kinds of sedimentary rock, the chief being **clay,** the particles of which are very fine ; **shale,** which is a clay that has become hard and splits easily ; and **slate,** also a clay, but which has undergone considerable changes due to pressure. It splits easily into slabs that are much more compact than in the case of shale.

Scenery depends to a great extent upon the nature of the rocks, and their arrangement. Sedimentary rocks, with the exception of limestone, give rise to landscapes differing greatly from those to be referred to in the next chapter. Hills are smooth in outline, and generally well clothed with vegetation.

Before leaving this subject we must refer to **coal,** though it is not a sediment. It occurs in beds which vary in thickness from one or two inches to thirty feet (in England), and fossilised leaves, branches and tree-trunks are found in great numbers, both in the coal and in the underlying bed, which is usually clay.

Coal is in fact compressed and mineralised vegetation, which grew ages ago in low-lying swamps.

Type of Scenery yielded by the softer Sedimentary Rocks
(Levisham.)

The land which supported it was sinking, and the vegetation, buried under a great mass of sediment, was subjected to enormous pressure which, aided by heat and moisture, produced the brittle, black rock called coal.

The vegetation must have been very luxuriant, and new growths must have sprung up in the sediments which covered the older ones, for coal-seams are found one above the other separated by beds of clay or sandstone.

The earth yields nothing which is of greater value to man than coal. Manufactures depend upon coal-supply, and all our great industrial towns are situated either on, or near to a coalfield. As examples, notice

A fractured Coal-seam. (Near Wakefield.)
The clay beneath the seam is more valuable than the coal; it is worked for the manufacture of bricks.

the great number of towns on the Lancashire coal-field, engaged in the manufacture of cotton goods; and on the other side of the Pennines, the busy towns of the West Riding of Yorkshire, which produce woollen goods, machinery and cutlery, using coal from the great coalfield which extends into four counties.

On the coalfields of the Midlands, pottery and iron goods are manufactured.

Britain has a rich supply of fuel, for there are ten important coal-basins in England in addition to a number of small ones, and five in Scotland. Iron-ore is found in most of these coal areas, a fortunate combination, for a plentiful supply of fuel is required for smelting the ore.

Coal is found in many countries of the European plain—chiefly in France and Germany—and in India, South Africa and Australia. In North America there are very large deposits, especially in the United States. China is believed to be the richest coal country in the world.

It must not be forgotten that the sedimentary rocks yield many other products of great value. Many sand-stones contain supplies of water, and the rock itself is useful as building-stone. Limestone is used in the manufacture of cement, and this rock often contains seams of lead-ore and zinc-ore.

Clay is made into bricks, tiles and earthenware. From shales is extracted oil, now a very valuable fuel. The chief oil-producing regions are the United States, the Caspian region, and the Anglo-Persian oil-fields near the Persian Gulf. The great demand for oil has brought fleets of oil-tankers on to the ocean routes.

At the surface, sedimentary rocks break up under the action of rain and frost, so forming a soil for the cultivation of crops. Agriculture is, of course, a more important occupation where minerals are scarce, or too far below the surface to be worked conveniently.

Thus the north and west of England are the great

mining and industrial areas, whilst the south and east are devoted chiefly to the raising of crops and the rearing of cattle.

EXERCISES

1. Make diagrams of sedimentary rocks (*a*) in horizontal position, (*b*) folded. (Sketch some that you have seen, if possible.)

2. Describe the appearance of sandstone, limestone, clay, and say what they are used for in industries.

3. Name some rocks which are porous, and some which are impervious to water. What will be the nature of the surface rocks where, after heavy rainfall, the land (*a*) dries quickly, (*b*) becomes marshy ?

4. What is meant by a coalfield ? Why are coalfields usually manufacturing areas ? On an outline map of the British Isles mark the position of our chief coalfields, and one or two important towns.

5. For what purposes is the Welsh "smokeless" coal specially valuable ?

IV. IGNEOUS ROCKS

In the last chapter it was pointed out that the surface rocks in England are mainly of the sedimentary type. In some parts of the country, however, there are rocks of an entirely different character. They occur in the Lake District, Wales, Cornwall, and also in the Highlands of Scotland ; districts which are noted for rugged scenery. From this you may rightly conclude that the rocks referred to have an influence on landscape-building.

The striking scenery of limestone areas is due largely to the solvent action of water. The wild

"Karst" Type of Scenery, near Ingleborough.

The Karst is a limestone plateau between the River Save and the Adriatic Sea. It is a region of gorges, caves and underground streams.

beauty of the regions named above is due to the presence of masses of very hard rock, which offer great resistance to the action of water.

It is easy to understand what will happen when rain and rivers work upon land which is composed of a mixture of sedimentary and these very hard rocks which are called **igneous.** The softer sediments will be worn away, whilst the igneous masses will stand boldly forth as hills or mountains, with deep irregular valleys between them.

Everyone is familiar with the appearance of granite, an igneous rock which is largely used for decorative purposes in building, and also, because of its hardness, as road-metal. You will have noticed that granite can be very highly polished, and more careful examination shows that it is composed of what for a moment we will call **fragments** of various colours. Sometimes it is possible to observe that these fragments which are so firmly welded into a compact mass, have certain very definite outlines. They are really **crystals** —one of the most beautiful products in nature.

Just in passing we may note that crystals are cut and mounted in the manufacture of jewellery. Quartz, one of the constituents of granite, amethyst, a coloured variety of quartz, ruby, sapphire, and many others are valued as gem-stones.

Igneous rocks, therefore, differ from the sedimentary rocks in two ways—they are harder, and they are crystalline. If we go into a quarry where igneous rock is being worked, we shall also notice that there is no parallel bedding.

It is evident then that these rocks have been formed in a special way, and to understand their mode

of formation we must know something about volcanoes.

A volcano is a mountain from which gases, including
water-vapour (steam), ashes, molten rock (lava) and
fragments of solid rock are ejected. There is no
fire, unless vegetation in the neighbourhood takes fire
from the red-hot lava ; but the glow from the molten

Friar's Crag, Derwentwater.

A promontory composed of igneous rock.   Softer sedimentary rocks
have been worn away from each side.

mass within the volcano is reflected by the cloud
which hangs above during an eruption, giving the
appearance of flames.

Though we have described a volcano as a "mountain," we must remember that an eruption may
break out in low-lying land, or even at the bottom of
the sea.   Huge quantities of lava and ashes are often

thrown out in a very short time. Long ago, in the year 79 A.D., two great cities, Pompeii and Herculaneum, were buried during an eruption of the Italian volcano, Vesuvius. Quite recently, in 1902, a terrible eruption occurred in the West Indies, when thousands of people lost their lives, suffocated by the vapours and fine dust which issued from the crater of Mont Pelée.

You will probably read more about these terrible displays of nature's force later. The interesting feature to us at present is that when lava has thoroughly cooled, it becomes hard. It may look like dark glass, or slag from a furnace, or crystalline, like many of the rocks which occur in our own country, and which we have called **igneous.**

In granite the crystals are larger than those which occur in beds of lava, and it is supposed that certain masses of molten rock became cool and solid, without ever reaching the surface of the earth. The cooling would therefore take place slowly, and big crystals would have time to build themselves. The presence of such a mass of rock in the earth is shown when water has worn away the softer rocks which concealed it.

We must conclude, then, that at some time in the past, active volcanoes have existed in Britain.

In the Lake District, in Wales and in the south-west of England they piled up great masses of lava and ashes which became consolidated, undergoing various changes in the process ; whilst at some places, Dartmoor, Shap Fells in Westmorland, and elsewhere, great blocks of granite were formed beneath the surface.

The Giant's Causeway, in the north of Ireland, is an

interesting feature. It is a small portion of a great outflow of lava, which, on cooling and solidifying, formed columns of solid rock with five or six sides.

You may observe that when the mud at the bottom of a pool becomes dry and hard, cracks divide it into pieces which are roughly hexagonal. The pieces are really columns, whose length is equal to the depth of

The Drying Bed of a Pool.

the layer of mud. In *this* case the contraction which splits the mud into columns is due to evaporation.

On the opposite side of the water which washes Giant's Causeway is Fingal's Cave, on the island of Staffa. The same kind of rock is to be seen there—it is another portion of the same flow of lava.

Our ancestors supposed that a causeway had been

built by giants across the sea, to enable kings and heroes to pass from one land to another. Hence the name.

Though it is many thousands of years since this lava was poured out on the earth's surface, it marks the most recent display of volcanic action in Britain.

The volcanic areas in our country have been subjected to the destructive process of **weathering** for

Giant's Causeway.

so long a period that it is not very easy to find exactly where the eruptions actually occurred. But worn down stumps of volcanoes have been discovered ; Arthur's Seat in Edinburgh is a well-known one.

You may have begun to wonder why the rocks we have been describing are called **igneous.**

Long ago people believed that a volcano was a burning mountain, that is, they thought that an eruption was caused by a fire raging within the mountain. Even in comparatively recent times some men have had the same idea, and supposed that an eruption occurred when coal-beds underground had caught fire.

The term **fire-rocks,** or igneous rocks (from the Latin word *ignis*, which means "fire"), therefore came into use. It may not be exactly suitable, but it is a convenient word and for that reason is still employed.

That there was some excuse for supposing an eruption to be due to fire, is shown by the following extract from a description of the eruption of Mont Pelée. "A red-hot avalanche rose from the cleft in the hill-side, and poured over the mountain slopes right down to the sea. It was dull red, and in it were bright streaks which we thought were large stones, as they seemed to give off tails of yellow sparks."

An eruption is probably due to the expansive force of steam, formed deep down in the earth, from water which has gradually made its way from the surface.

At any rate, we know that the interior of the earth is very hot, and water which descended very far would be converted into steam, which would force a passage through any weak part of the earth's **crust.**

We may note here that hot springs, called **geysers,** are common in districts where volcanoes have become **extinct.** Very fine examples are found, as we mentioned in a previous chapter, in the Yellowstone Park of America. Others are known in Iceland, New Zealand and Japan.

We must briefly refer to certain rocks which extend over a great area in the Scottish Highlands.

They resemble the sedimentary rocks in that they have a banded structure, but they are crystalline like the igneous rocks. It is supposed that they were once ordinary sediments ; but having been buried under later deposits and subjected to great pressure and heat, they were changed into crystalline rocks.

The **change of form** which they have undergone is indicated by their name **metamorphic rocks.** They are to be seen in almost every country. They form the central part or core of most of the world's great mountain systems—the Alps, the Himalayas, and the Rockies, and give rise to scenery of a most magnificent kind. But they are found in lower ground also, and in such cases they have probably been greatly worn by climatic influences and by rivers.

Igneous and metamorphic rocks do not give a land-surface which is fit for cultivation ; but the hills and mountains which they build can often be used as pasture-lands.

Still these rocks are extremely rich in metallic ores, which in the course of time are separated and stored elsewhere by water, as in the case of the gold-bearing sands and gravels of South Africa, Klondike, and Australia, or the tin-bearing alluvium of the Malay Peninsula. The tin-workings of the Malay States are the richest in the world, they supply more than half the tin-ore used. From what has been said you will understand how during past ages metals have found a place in sedimentary rocks.

During and after a volcanic eruption also, cracks which have been formed in the surrounding rocks are filled up with ore by metal-bearing water or vapour, coming up from the interior of the earth.

You will therefore expect to find stores of useful
minerals in the neighbourhood of igneous rocks.
This is quite correct.   In Cornwall, for example, veins
of copper, tin, iron and lead are very numerous ;
they lie around the granite masses.

Alluvial Tin-workings, Malay States.

The metamorphic rocks of Scandinavia are very
rich in silver-ore and iron-ore.   The latter has long
been exported to England for smelting.

In America the same type of rock extends over a
great area around Hudson's Bay, and contains great
beds of iron-ore.   Enormous quantities of this ore
are mined near Lake Superior and sent to ports on the
southern shore.

EXERCISES

1. Draw a map of Sicily and southern Italy. Mark the positions of the volcanoes Vesuvius, Stromboli and Etna.

Whereabouts are the volcanic peaks Hecla and Erebus ?

2. Why is granite largely used in road-making and the construction of docks and breakwaters ?

Why is it used for "facing" buildings ?

3. Igneous rocks are sometimes instrumental in causing waterfalls. Make a diagram to show the part they play.

4. What is the character of the scenery in areas where igneous rocks occur ? Name such areas in Britain.

V. HIGHLANDS AND LOWLANDS

We have already mentioned the fact that beds of sedimentary rock do not always occupy a horizontal position, and you will have many opportunities of verifying this if you inspect quarries, or, when you travel by train, the sides of a railway cutting. You will probably find cases in which the beds form an arch or a trough.

Evidently some force has acted on the sediments after they became solidified, causing them to crumple up.

Place a number of sheets of paper in a neat pile on the table. Then, with a hand on each of two opposite edges, force these edges towards each other.

The resulting folds are exactly similar to those shown by the folded sedimentary rocks.

This simple experiment suggests that the beds, so carefully laid down by water, have been bent and crumpled by some compressing force. This is quite true. Our earth was formerly a very hot globe consisting of molten material only. The outermost layers have cooled so far as to become solid, and to submit to all the processes described in previous chapters.

The interior of the earth is still very hot, and is probably partly in the molten state. But it is

Folded Beds of Limestone, near Bolton Abbey (Yorks.).

gradually becoming cooler, and is therefore becoming smaller.

The hard outer layer, which is called the **earth's crust,** has in consequence to fit itself to a diminishing interior, and so wrinkles or folds are produced.

Perhaps this will remind you that the skin of an apple, which has been kept for a long time in a dry place, becomes very wrinkled. The explanation is that the interior of the apple has been shrinking, in consequence of loss of moisture, and the skin has to adjust itself to the reduced bulk. But though this furnishes a good illustration of the production of wrinkles in an outer layer, by the contraction of the interior, the process is much more rapid, and the effects are more strongly marked, than in the case of the earth.

The folds in the crust of the earth were not produced suddenly. They are the result of movements extending over thousands of years. It is even believed that some **wrinkles,** whose formation commenced long before man appeared on the earth, are not yet complete, though the movement of the crust is proceeding so gradually that it is not perceived.

Sometimes, however, the rocks are subjected to so great a strain in the folding process, that they break asunder. Movement of a violent nature follows—we call it **earthquake.** One portion of the land may be thrust upward, whilst an adjoining area may be depressed. Such a fracture is shown in the photograph on page 31, the left-hand portion of the coal is depressed. Even though a slip of this kind be not more than a foot, much damage may be done.

Examples of folding and fracture are very numerous in the Pennines. In quarries and railway cuttings, the beds of limestone or sandstone are found tilted, and sometimes bent into upfolds and downfolds ; whilst lines of fracture are found in great numbers, especially on the western side.

We must remember that a fracture in the rocks only appears to be a **line** at the surface—just as a

crack in an earthenware vessel shows its presence by a
line on the surface of the earthenware. We know
then that the Pennines are a system of mountains
produced by the folding and uplifting of a portion of
the earth's crust. After the uplift had taken place,
water proceeded with its task of wearing away the

Upfolds and Downfolds in Sedimentary Rocks, near Skipton.

land, and, aided by frost, wind, and wind-borne dust,
removed much sediment to lower ground. The process
has continued for ages, with the result that huge
mountain blocks have been carved out. To these,
distinctive names have been given, e.g. Ingleborough

In the south-west of England, the Mendip Hills furnish another example of a fold. They are part of a long **wrinkle,** which extends from Ireland, through England, and far away into the continent, through the Harz Mountains of Germany.

All the great mountain systems in the world have been formed in the same way. The Scottish Grampians

Ingleborough.

and the Scandinavian mountains were formed long before the uplift of the Pennines. The great land area of Eurasia is traversed by a number of mountain systems—the Alps, Himalayas, etc., which were built at a much later date. Being "young" they are lofty. In the course of time their altitude will be reduced by water and other agents. Many Asiatic systems

radiate from the high Pamir Plateau—the "Roof of
the World."

Other systems of fold mountains stretch along
the eastern side of the Pacific from Alaska to Cape
Horn, the chief members being the Rockies and the
Andes. But you will notice that these huge systems
consist of a series of lofty ridges almost parallel to
each other. Try to imagine the nature of the course
one would follow in making a journey across North
America. It would be something like the line between
A and *B* in this figure. There would be similar

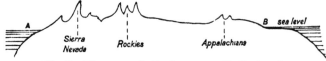

Fig. 7.   Diagrammatic Section across North America.

variations in altitude during the course of a journey
across the mountain systems of Asia, and again, but
less marked, in South America.

It appears then that the biggest wrinkles in the
earth's crust have formed huge troughs, occupied by
the oceans, and great uplifts which we call continents;
and that the land-surfaces have been thrust into a
number of smaller wrinkles, producing mountain-
systems and lowlands. From the high land flow
streams, constantly engaged in cutting up the masses,
and bearing the waste material down through the
valleys towards the ocean. The mountain systems
are therefore **continental water-partings**, dividing the
waters they receive between the distant oceans.

Throughout the greater portion of the earth's
history, some part or other of the crust has been under-

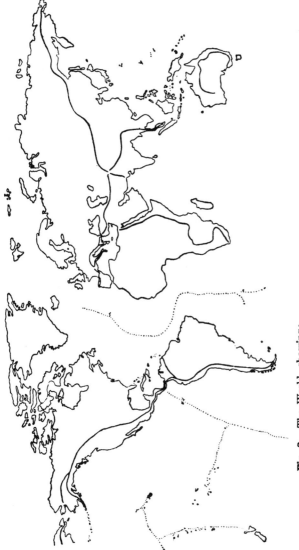

Fig. 8. The World, showing:

(a) Direction of continental water-partings.

(b) Chief submarine ridges and the islands situated on them.

going the process of folding, but there are some hard blocks which have offered great resistance. Wales, the Highlands of Scotland, the Iberian Peninsula, and Bohemia, are such blocks. They have served as buttresses against which softer rocks have folded. Place one hand firmly on the cloth which covers a table, and with the other push the cloth along the table. In this way you may illustrate the part played by these blocks, which, though they are not peaks, are called "crust-block mountains."

Before leaving the subject of "highlands," we must notice that volcanic action accounts for the formation of **groups** of mountains. The ashes, lava, etc., which are ejected during an eruption are piled up in a conical mass around the crater, and if action is proceeding at a number of different points in the area, an irregular group of volcanic peaks is built up. This has occurred in the Lake District—the Cumbrian Group, and in the central part of France.

We must also note that volcanic action does not take place on land only. In the Pacific Ocean particularly, outbursts have occurred on the ocean floor, and the mountains which were built up in that way project above the surface of the water as islands. Such is the origin of the Hawaii Group.

Now it is quite clear that when mountains are formed, either by the wrinkling of the earth's crust or by volcanic action, low-lying land, **valleys,** must lie between the wrinkles and between the peaks. But whatever the surface of the land may be like, it is certain to be modified by rivers.

You know that they are always wearing away the rocks. They flow from high ground along the valleys,

Grisedale Tarn, Dollywaggon Pike (2810 ft.), St Sunday Crag (2756 ft.), and, in the distance, Ullswater. All the hills and mountains in this area are composed of volcanic rocks. They form part of the Cumbrian "group," though most of them lie within the Westmorland boundary.

which they are constantly making deeper. In addition to separating massive blocks from a long upfold, as we have already mentioned, they make for themselves channels across those high and extensive tracts of land called crust-block mountains, thus carving out mountains, hills and valleys, from what may have been an almost level area. Examine physical maps and you will see how Wales, the Highlands, Spain, and Bohemia have been dissected by rivers.

Rivers are very powerful valley-makers, but they are greatly assisted by rain, which softens the rocks, and by frost, which, by freezing water that has trickled into narrow crevices, loosens large blocks.

Glaciers, i.e. ice-rivers, also have a share in carving the surface of the earth; we shall consider their work in the next chapter.

But there are certain valleys which are indirectly due to the action of rivers. You will remember that in some areas rivers frequently flow underground, and that the roof of the channel thus made sometimes collapses. It may, however, sink downwards to some extent, thus forming on the surface a long hollow which is called a **dry valley**. Of course, if a river deserts its old channel in favour of an underground route, a similar valley will result, without any subsidence.

Dry valleys are quite common in districts where the rocks are limestone or chalk.

A totally different kind of valley is that formed by the subsidence of a belt of land, between those great cracks which are so often made in the earth's crust during the process of folding. It is called a **rift-valley.**

The Central Valley of Scotland, which lies between the Highlands and the Southern Uplands, is an

Dry Valley, Gordale.

example, but there is a still greater one in Palestine—the valley of the river Jordan. This is prolonged towards the central region of Africa, where it is partly occupied by great lakes.

But there are large tracts of land which possess neither mountain nor valley of any importance. The eastern part of England is such an area, and it is continued across northern Europe and Siberia, except for the break at the Ural Mountains. Across these **plains** rivers flow slowly ; but in times of flood a rush of water takes place over the flat land, and a thin layer of sediment is deposited. In such a way plains near the sea have been built up. They are areas of deposition.

The plains of the world are therefore formed of gravel and sand which has been carried from the mountains. It must be noted that when a river overflows, sediment is deposited in greatest quantity nearest to the channel, so that the banks are gradually raised above the level of the land on each side ; and as the river is moving slowly, instead of deepening its channel, it is depositing sediment on its bed. Thus the river itself is being raised. A most interesting case is the Po, which with its tributaries has built the plain of Lombardy with material from the Alps. In some places the river is above the level of the adjacent houses, and is banked up with dykes to prevent disastrous floods.

Mountain systems are often a serious hindrance to communication between different parts of a country, for the construction of railways over high ground is difficult, and heavy trains cannot be drawn up a steep incline. The direction of the routes between London and Scotland is governed by the Pennines. Look at your map, and trace the East Coast route through the Vale of York, and northwards near the coast; and the West Coast route through the Lancashire plain, and then, after the steep ascent of Shap Fells, down the Eden and up the Nith valley towards Glasgow. Often the costly work of tunnel-making must be undertaken. The Alps have been pierced in several places. The Simplon tunnel is over 12 miles long, and its construction occupied seven years. The

A Pass in the Pennines. (Buttertubs near Hawes.)

Loetschberg tunnel, which was opened for passenger traffic in July 1913, is nine miles long, and six years were spent in making it.

Whenever possible valleys are taken as the route through a mountain system.

Roads and railways are carried from valley to valley over the lowest part of the ridge which separates them, called a **pass**. Some of the passes in the Rocky Mountains, traversed by the Canadian railways, are, however, very far above sea-level; Kicking Horse Pass, for example, has an altitude of 5000 feet.

Communication between the east and west of the Pennines is rendered easy by a break in the mountains

A Gap in the Chilterns, near Princes Risborough.

called the **Aire Gap**. Through it have been constructed the L.M. & S. railway and the Leeds and Liverpool canal.

You will notice also that many gaps in the chalk ridge have been of great service to builders of railways. On referring to your map you will find that branches of the L. & N.E., L.M. & S., and G.W. railways pass through Chiltern gaps at Hitchin, Luton, Tring and

Princes Risborough respectively. In Scotland, the Grampians are crossed by the L.M. & S. Railway, via the valleys of the Tay, the Garry, and the Spey.

EXERCISES

1. Make rough diagrams to show the variation in altitude across England (*a*) from St Bees Head to Flamborough Head ; (*b*) from Holyhead to Chelmsford. Write the names uplift, ridge, vale, plain, etc., over the features represented.

2. Make diagrams to show the variation in altitude (*a*) across the African plateau, eastwards from the mouth of the Congo ; (*b*) from Cape Comorin (India) northwards across the Deccan plateau, Ganges valley, Himalayas, plateau of Tibet, Desert of Gobi, Altai Mountains and Siberian plain. Name all these features.

3. On an outline map of England indicate the chief water-partings by means of a thick line for the well-marked ones, and a dotted line for those that are ill-defined.

4. Write out a list of countries in Europe which are separated from others by mountain systems. Make rough diagrams to illustrate, and show the chief lines of communication across the mountains.

5. On an outline map of England, draw lines to show the direction of the oolitic ridge and the chalk ridge. Use a dotted line where the ridge is broken.

VI. WORK DONE BY ICE

In England the temperature of the air is sometimes so low that the moisture in the atmosphere freezes and falls as snow or hail.

Over the greater part of the earth snow is unknown. In temperate lands it falls in winter only, whilst in the polar regions it may fall throughout the year. But as we ascend from the surface of the earth, the air becomes colder, and it is possible everywhere to reach a layer of the atmosphere which is at freezing point.

On all high mountains, such as the Alps and Himalayas, there is a line, called the **snow-line,** above which snow never melts.

In the hot regions of the earth, the snow-line is naturally higher than in other parts. In the Himalayas it is from 15,000 to 20,000 feet above sea-level. In the Alps it is from 8500 to 9000 feet, while in Spitzbergen it is only 1000 feet up. No British mountains quite reach the snow-line.

On lofty mountains, and on lower ground in polar regions, the layer of snow attains a great thickness. On steep slopes huge masses sometimes become detached, rush down the mountain side, increasing in size and speed as they descend, and sweep away rocks, trees and other obstructions which may be in their path. Such a mass is called an **avalanche.**

In Switzerland belts of forest have been planted for the purpose of protecting villages and cultivated land from the destructive action of avalanches.

But there is another process by which snow passes from the mountain top to lower ground, a movement as slow as that of the avalanche is swift. Great expanses of snow are converted into ice by the pressure of the thick layer, and begin to move slowly down the valleys as ice-rivers or **glaciers.**

From the smaller valleys on each side of a larger one issue other glaciers, tributaries of the main one.

More snow is constantly being piled up on the higher ground, so that, though the lower end of the

Mt Cook, the highest point in the Southern Alps, New Zealand. The summit is over 2000 ft. above the snow-line.

glacier melts away when it reaches a warmer region, there is no interruption of the flow of the ice-river.

When you break ice which has formed over a very shallow pool, you may notice earth adhering to the under surface. Glaciers possess this power of picking up earth in a high degree.

In addition, from the high ground which is free

Upper Arolla Glacier.

from snow on each side of the valley, other material is constantly falling down, spreading over the surface of the ice, and in particular forming along the sides of the glacier lines of rocks and earth called **moraines**.

When two glaciers join there will be a moraine along the middle of the enlarged glacier.

Blocks of rock frequently fall into **crevasses**— great cracks formed when the glacier is passing over the uneven valley floor, and, becoming embedded in the base of the ice, make deep furrows in the ground over which they are dragged.

Quite recently glaciers in Spitzbergen have been carefully examined, and it has been found that they plough up the ground and push forward great quantities

Glacier Table. (Upper Arolla Glacier.)

When a slab of rock falls upon a glacier it protects the ice beneath it from the sun's rays, and so in the course of time is poised on a pedestal of ice. Notice that the table is tilted, because the ice melts more rapidly on one side (south) than on the other.

of earth, much of which they pick up later. Ice therefore takes an important part in the work of valley-making.

A glacier continues its advance until it reaches a point where the rate of melting equals that of the movement of the ice. Consequently in Switzerland glaciers may be seen with cultivated land on each side. The great glaciers of the Southern Alps in New

Crossing a Crevasse, Upper Arolla Glacier.

Zealand descend into the forested portion of the mountains, to within 1000 feet of sea-level.

From the end of a glacier flows a stream carrying still further much of the earthy debris which the ice contained.

The Rhone is such a river. Its source is a glacier on Mont St Gothard, whence it flows as a muddy stream to Lake Geneva.

In the Arctic and Antarctic regions, glaciers continue their journey to the coast and glide into the sea. Then large blocks break off and float away as **icebergs.** From the Arctic they travel far into the

Stream issuing from the foot of Arolla Glacier. Morainic material lies on each side.

Atlantic Ocean, and are often seen from ships, towering a hundred feet or more above the surface of the water.

Since ice floats with only one-ninth of its mass above water, such blocks must be about a thousand feet thick.

The presence of icebergs in the North Atlantic during the spring months makes navigation dangerous.

In 1912, collision with an iceberg caused the loss of the greatest ocean liner, the *Titanic*.

The climate of Britain must once have been much colder than it is now, for though there is no human record of the existence of glaciers in our land, the work they have done can be seen in many places.

In all parts of Britain north of the Thames valley, a layer of **boulder-clay** is found above the solid sedimentary rocks. It consists of earth and fragments of rock, some of which are scratched, and so strongly resembles the material which forms moraines in the Alpine glaciers, that we may be sure it has been deposited by melting ice-rivers.

Scratches on the rocks in valleys and on mountain slopes indicate the direction taken by the glaciers. Large pieces of rock have been found miles away from their natural home. Granite, for example, has been transported from Shap Fells, west of the Pennines, through a gap in the mountains and down the valley of the Tees to the Yorkshire coast.

In the mountainous parts of the country, almost every valley must have had its glacier. Over the north and central parts of Europe and North America there is abundant evidence of the presence of ice during the same period—a period now described as the **Great Ice Age.**

The story of this age is one of the strangest in the earth's history, only equalled by what we learn from the discovery of coal in the Arctic and Antarctic regions. These lands, now fast bound by snow and ice, once enjoyed a climate which favoured the development of luxuriant vegetation.

Soil, in which crops are raised, is formed by the

decomposition of the upper surface of sedimentary rocks, and its nature will therefore depend on the rock from which it is formed. But you will now see that

Boulder-clay, resting on limestone. (Teesdale.)

the soil cultivated in many parts of the country is boulder-clay. This forms a valuable soil, for it is composed of materials collected by glaciers during their progress over different kinds of rock.

EXERCISES

1. In what countries and which mountain systems do glaciers exist ? Give the names of any glaciers you have heard of.

2. Make a diagram to show the junction of two glaciers, and the union of two lateral moraines to form a medial moraine.

3. How are icebergs formed ? Show by means of a sketch how an iceberg floats in water. What becomes of the boulders, etc. when the iceberg melts ?

4. Mention some facts which show that glaciers once existed in England.

VII. CLIMATIC ZONES

From the last chapter you would learn that the glaciers on the earth's surface are found either in the polar regions or in lofty mountain systems of warmer lands.

Our English climate does not favour the formation of glaciers ; for though in winter we sometimes have severe weather, during the greater part of the year snow never falls.

You are familiar with the gradual change from the **short days** of winter to the **long days** of summer ; and you will have noticed that the sun's rays appear to have smaller heating power in winter.

We cannot suppose there is any change in the sun himself, so we must seek an explanation of the change from winter cold to summer heat in the way the sun's heat is conveyed to the earth.

Perhaps you have already observed that the sun reaches his highest position on any day at noon.

Take a rod, say a foot long. Place it upright in the ground, and measure the shadow cast by the sun, each hour from 9 a.m. to 3 p.m.

The first thing you notice probably is that the direction of the shadow is constantly changing ; and if on a summer day you observe the 6 a.m. and the 6 p.m. shadows you will find them pointing in exactly opposite directions. During 12 hours the shadow has rotated through 180°. This indicates that the earth has made a half-turn on its axis. It will remind you too that other places, previously in darkness, have

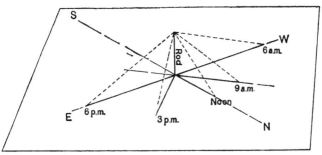

Fig. 9. Changes in length of shadow of rod.

been brought within range of the sun's rays, and that a place half-way round the world from where we are will have its noon when we have midnight. A difference in longitude of 180° is therefore equivalent to 12 hours in time, or 15° to one hour. It follows that St Louis (90° W.) and Dacca (90° E.) will have noon at 6 p.m. and 6 a.m. respectively, according to English time.

But now let us consider the lengths of the shadows, and what they indicate. You find that the shortest shadow is the one measured at noon. The line which joins the end of the shadow to the top of the rod gives the direction of the sun's rays ; and as you see from Fig. 9, a short shadow denotes greater altitude of the sun than a long one.

When we speak of the summer or winter altitude of the sun, you must remember that the midday altitude is meant.

Now take your one-foot rod, and fix it upright in the centre of a board.   Find a place where there is nothing to block out the sunlight, and place the board there, in a perfectly level position.

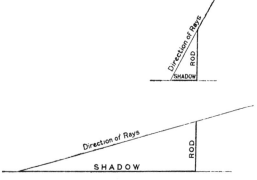

Fig. 10.   Shadows on June 21 and Dec. 21

The length of the rod's shadow must now be measured once a week, at midday on Mondays, say, from June to December.   Enter the readings taken in a notebook.

From these readings you may construct diagrams like those in Fig. 10, indicating the direction of the sun's rays.

It is plain that on December 21 the rays are much nearer the horizontal than they are on June 21.

Let us now make diagrams to show how a *bundle* of rays strikes the ground on June 21st and on December 21st (Fig. 11).

The parallel lines in the figures (each group measures 7 mm. across), represent a section, i.e. the distance *through* the bundle.

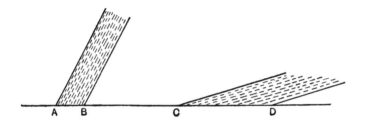

Area heated by bundle
of rays (June)

Area heated by bundle of rays
(December)

Fig. 11. Areas heated in June and December.

You notice that *CD*, the length of line intercepted in the December diagram, is much greater than *AB*. If on *AB* and *CD* as axes, ellipses are described, we obtain the areas heated by equal cylindrical bundles of rays, in June and in December.

By measurement we find the axis of one ellipse is over three times the axis of the other; therefore the *area* of the big ellipse is three times that of the smaller.

If the equal bundles convey equal quantities of heat, any portion of the small ellipse, say *P*, will receive three times as much heat as the equal portion *Q* of the bigger area. The fact is, however, that the December rays lose more heat than the June rays in travelling from sun to earth, because they have a longer journey through the atmosphere (Fig. 11*a*).

Our winter temperature is, therefore, lower than that of summer, because (1) the winter rays travel

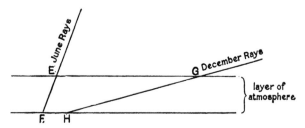

Fig. 11 *a*. *GH* is nearly four times as long as *EF*.

more obliquely and their influence is therefore distributed over a greater area ; (2) the winter rays are actually more feeble when they reach the earth than the summer ones are.

There is a third reason, which you know quite well. In summer the sun is above the horizon for a much longer period per day than he is in winter.

But effects due to changes in the slope of sun-rays may be observed during a single day. At noon the sun reaches his greatest altitude, the path of the rays is then steepest, and the earth is receiving heat at the greatest rate.

In the morning and in the evening, when the sun is near the horizon, the rays are almost horizontal, and they have little effect upon the surface of the land.

Now if we could be at some place on the tropic of Cancer on June 21, or on the tropic of Capricorn on December 21, we should find the sun's rays descending from the **zenith**—the point overhead. What we have already discovered will enable you to decide that such rays—vertical ones, must have the maximum heating effect. You will find a vivid description of tropical noon in *The Ancient Mariner*.

Between June 21 and December 21, successive belts of that portion of the earth's surface which lies between the tropics, receive vertical rays; and they have the same experience again between December 21 and June 21. The equator has its turn on September 23 and March 21. Even during the rest of the year, the rays never strike the earth at an angle less than 43°, and this region, the **torrid zone**, is the hottest part of the earth's surface.

On the other hand, lands further north than Britain receive the rays more slantingly than we do on any particular day. This is more and more pronounced the further we go northwards, and the same holds for the southern hemisphere. At the poles the sun's rays are never more than $23\frac{1}{2}°$ from the horizontal—and that occurs only on one day, June 21 for the north pole, December 21 for the south pole. For six months of the year no sunlight at all reaches the poles.

The cause of the changes in the direction of the sun's rays we will not consider now. That is a little problem which may be postponed for a while. But it will be clear to you that the equatorial belt of the earth has a very hot climate ; and that, advancing northwards, or southwards, there is a **temperate zone**, where summer and winter occur—the former not very hot, and the latter not very cold. Then

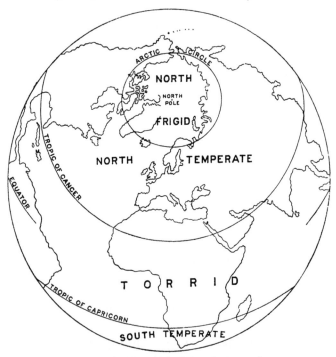

Fig. 12. The Land Hemisphere—Climatic Zones.

there is a **north frigid**, and a **south frigid** zone, lying around the poles. Parts of these have short summers and long severe winters, but as the poles are approached the climate changes to everlasting winter. You must remember also that during our summer it is winter in the southern hemisphere.

Though it is convenient to speak of climatic "zones," we must remember there is no sharp line of division between one zone and the next. Tropical conditions gradually yield to temperate, and a temperate climate imperceptibly gives place to Arctic cold as the poles are approached. Sudden changes *do* occur in nature, but they are contrary to the rule.

The rule holds with regard to lofty mountains in the torrid zone, the Himalayas, the Andes and the African peaks. The low land in these regions has a very hot climate ; but, ascending the mountain slopes, there is a gradual change from tropical heat to polar cold. Exactly those types of climate are experienced which are encountered between the torrid zone and the poles. The "snow-line" is passed on the northern side of the Himalayas at an altitude of 19,000 feet, and above this the ground is always covered with snow.

The tops of such mountains reach those altitudes where the air is **thin,** or, to use a more exact expression, the **density** of the air is very small. People who ascend such high mountains find great difficulty in breathing, for this reason. Sir Ernest Shackleton, in *The Heart of the Antarctic*, tells how the members of the expedition suffered from mountain-sickness, and bleeding from the nose, when travelling on the plateau 10,000 feet above the sea.

These higher layers of atmosphere are scarcely affected by the sun-warmed earth, and such heat-rays as do reach them pass through the **thin** air very easily, producing very little rise in temperature.

We must not, however, suppose that lands of equal altitude, even in the same climatic zone, have always

The Cascade Mountains.

Illustrating the effect of altitude on climate. This region has about the same latitude as Essex, but its vegetation resembles that of the north of Scotland.

similar climates. Let us consider the case of two cities, Moscow and Edinburgh. They are both in the north temperate zone, they are at equal distances from the equator (i.e. they have the same latitude) and they have the same altitude.

But, as you probably know, the winter is much more severe in Moscow than it is in Edinburgh ; men

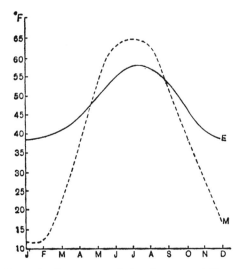

Fig. 13. Range in Temperature during the year, at Moscow and at Edinburgh; plotted from Tables of Average Monthly Temperature.

are in the habit of wearing coats lined with fur or sheep's wool. In summer, the weather is distinctly hotter in Moscow than in the Scottish capital. Stating the conditions in figures, the Edinburgh temperature varies from 38° in January to 58° in July—*a range of* 20° ; whilst the Moscow readings are 12° in January and 65° in July—*a range of* 53°.

This remarkable difference must be explained by the difference in situation of the two cities. Moscow is in the middle of a great land mass, far from the sea ; Edinburgh is on an island (Great Britain) and is close to the sea. Now heat is absorbed by water more slowly than by land, and land cools more

62°—64°

60°—62°

55°—60°

Fig. 14. Isotherm Map of the British Isles (July).

rapidly than water does. Consequently, during the summer, land becomes hotter than the adjacent waters, but later on loses heat at such a rate that it soon becomes cooler than the sea.

Places near the sea are therefore warmed in winter and cooled in summer, by air from the sea passing over the land. Towns like Moscow which are remote from the coast miss these tempering influences; and having these extremes of heat and cold, their climate is termed **extreme,** or with reference to the cause, **continental**.

The temperatures mentioned above are the average

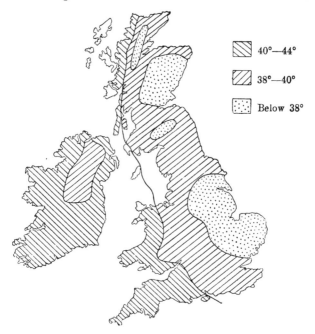

40°—44°

38°—40°

Below 38°

Fig. 15. Isotherm Map of the British Isles (January).

temperatures for the months named, i.e. the average of the daily readings throughout the month. The average monthly temperature for a great number of places all over the world has been found. You might find a number of places having the same temperature for a certain month, say July. Now if on a map you draw a line joining all those places, you would have an **equal-heat** line, or, to use the proper name, an **isotherm.** Isotherm maps are of great service. When you examine those of the British Isles, you learn that in January places on a line extending from Cape Wrath southwards to the Isle of Wight, have the same temperature 40°— a remarkable testimony to the influence of the Atlantic Ocean on the climate of Britain. Equally interesting features are shown by the isotherm maps of the continent, and the world, but we will not consider them now.

The difference in heat-absorbing power of land and water, referred to above, has some important consequences. On a hot day the air over the land becomes heated, and therefore lighter, and it passes upwards. This causes an inflow of cooler air from the sea. The current gradually increases in strength, forming a **sea-breeze,** but begins to die down during the afternoon, when the temperature of the sea is approaching that of the land. As the sun sinks towards the horizon, the land becomes cooler and cooler, and during the night the conditions are reversed. A **land-breeze** blows from the land to the warmer sea.

Some lands in the torrid zone experience **monsoon winds** which are produced in the same way as sea-breezes, but operate over a *season*. They are well-marked in India. The land is highly heated during the six months the sun is north of the equator (from March 21 to September 23), and has no opportunity to become cool.

From about April to October, the monsoon blows

from the sea, bearing much moisture which falls as rain.

If the monsoon fails there is great distress in the country, for India depends upon the monsoon for the watering of her crops.

The conditions are reversed during the rest of the year, and the wind blows from the land seawards. It is sometimes called the **dry monsoon.**

We must now consider what follows from the difference in temperature of the various climatic *belts* of the earth's surface. We will confine our attention to the ocean, because land areas introduce complications which we do not wish to consider at this stage.

That part of the ocean which lies near the equator is always very warm. Here then the air will constantly be rising, so that we might call this a **low pressure belt.**

High pressure belts will of course lie, one on each side of the low pressure area ; and from them there is a steady movement of air towards the equator, causing **constant winds** named the **Trades.**

Now if the earth were stationary these winds would blow from north to south in the northern hemisphere, and from south to north in the southern.

But you will have learned that our round earth revolves upon its axis, and so be prepared to hear that the direction of the winds is affected.

The result is a **north-east trade-wind** in the northern, and a **south-east trade-wind** in the southern hemisphere. To illustrate this change in direction, set a globe with a blackboard surface spinning, and try to draw a line from one of the poles directly towards the equator.

The name **trade** has been applied to these winds for a very long time. It is commonly said that the name has reference to the service rendered to trade by the winds, when steamships were unknown ; but other explanations have been given. Between the trade-wind belts there is a region of " calms "—the equatorial calms, also known as the **Doldrums**. In the days of sailing-vessels, this belt was dreaded by sailors, for ships were often becalmed for a long time, " as idle as a painted ship, upon a painted ocean."

From the high pressure belts named, air moves towards the poles as well as towards the equator, so that we get two other systems of constant winds. They also are deflected, and appear to blow from the south-west in the northern hemisphere, and from the north-west in the southern.

Often they are called the **westerly winds**. Sometimes they are described as the **antitrades**, because they blow in directions opposed to those of the trades, but the former is the better name.

In the southern hemisphere there are few land masses, and the westerly winds are remarkably steady, receiving for this reason the description **Brave West Winds.**

Earlier in this chapter it was noted that the poles have darkness for six months. During the rest of the year they have continuous daylight. We cannot discover this for ourselves, but we have the evidence of men who have been there.

In June, 1914, Sir Ernest Shackleton describing the work to be done by the Antarctic expedition, said, " As there will be broad daylight during the whole of the five months the expedition is on the march, the ordinary day of 24 hours will be disregarded, and a new one of 19 hours established."

We who have never been in the polar regions are likely to forget that there is not at the poles the

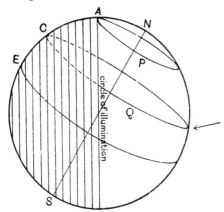

Fig. 16.   Illumination of the Earth on June 21.

The arrow does not indicate the direction of the sun's rays, but the point where they fall vertically.

"Circle of illumination" is a convenient term for the boundary between the dark and illuminated halves of the globe, though really there is no sharp line of division.

Notice that the Arctic circle (*AP*) is entirely within the illuminated half. Any point, *P*, on this circle therefore has daylight during a complete revolution of the earth; whilst *Q*, on the tropic of Cancer, has more daylight than darkness in the 24 hours. It is midday at the north pole; and the sun will not set until the circle of illumination creeps back to *N*, as shown in the next figure.

frequent alternation of light and darkness, which is such an aid to us in England in dividing our time. Light first reaches the south pole on Sept. 23, when the sun has reached the equator on his southward journey; and during the time occupied by the sun in travelling from the equator to the tropic of Capricorn, and back again to the equator, there is daylight at the south pole.

Before going further, you must remember that we are speaking of the sun's *apparent* journey. The journeys he seems to make between the tropics are due to the movements of our earth.

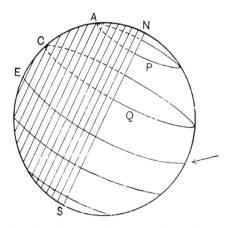

Fig. 17. Illumination of the Earth at the Equinoxes—
Sept. 23 and Mar. 21.

The circle of illumination passes through the poles, bisecting the Arctic circle, tropic of Cancer, and every other parallel of latitude. *P*, *Q*, and all other places on the earth have therefore 12 hours daylight and 12 hours darkness during a revolution of the globe.

On Sept. 23, it is sunset at the north pole and sunrise at the south pole.

Well, each day after Sept. 23, the sun has moved a little further south, and at the south pole he will appear each day a little higher above the horizon. This continues until Dec. 21, when the sun, having reached the tropic of Capricorn, begins to go northward.

On March 21, the south pole night begins, and the north pole night ends. Then whilst the sun travels to the tropic of Cancer and back again to the equator, the north pole has **day**, and the south pole has **night**. The long stretch of daylight does not mean that much heat is given to the polar regions ; the rays strike the earth in a direction little removed from the horizontal.

Places near the poles will have long midwinter **nights** and long midsummer **days**. This becomes

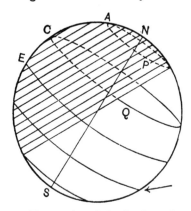

Fig. 18. Illumination of the Earth on Dec. 21.
The sun is not seen from any point within the Arctic circle; and *Q* is longer in darkness than in light during 24 hours.

less marked as distance from the poles increases. On June 21, sunset at Lerwick (Shetlands) occurs at 9.30 p.m. ; at London, 8.18 p.m. You have heard Norway described as the " Land of the Midnight Sun." Hammerfest, in the north of Norway, has a midsummer **day**, i.e. period of daylight, extending over nine weeks.

The diagrams will help to make the matter clearer.

EXERCISES

1. Name places where the sun is (a) never seen in the north ; (b) never seen in the south ; (c) never seen in the north during one part of the year and never seen in the south during the remaining months.

2. When it is noon at Greenwich, what will be the time at a place exactly half-way round the world [i.e., 180° W. (or E) longitude] ; at New Orleans (90° W.) and at Dacca (90° E.) ?

3. Bridgewater in Somersetshire and Bootle (Liverpool) have noon at the same time. State the position of Bootle with regard to Bridgewater. From your map find the meridian on which they are situated, and name other pairs of towns which have noon at the same instant.

4. At noon on March 21, two persons A and B, stationed at different points on the earth's surface, see the sun on the horizon ; C observes that it is in the zenith, and D finds that it is 40° above the horizon. State the positions of A, B, C and D. What will each person observe on succeeding days ?

5. The mean monthly temperatures at Vancouver and Winnipeg are given in the table :

V.	34	35	44	47	55	58	60	65	57	50	43	36
W.	−5	0	15	38	52	63	68	64	53	40	20	5

Find the annual range at each place and explain the difference. Show the variation during the year by means of a diagram.

VIII. THE SEA

The great hollows in the earth's crust are occupied by seas and oceans which, connected one with another, form one vast sheet of water covering three-quarters of the earth's surface.

The seas around the British Isles are comparatively shallow. In few places is the North Sea more than 300 feet deep, whilst the Dogger Bank, which lies between England and Denmark, is in some parts less than 100 feet below the surface.

Passing westwards from the British Isles, a rapid increase in depth is noticed about 200 miles from the Irish coast. The bed of the sea descends suddenly to a thousand fathoms.

This indicates the edge of the great hollow or trough which lies between the Old World and the New, and is occupied by the Atlantic Ocean.

Between America and Asia is another even greater ocean trough, the Pacific. Both these oceans extend northwards to the Arctic, and southwards to the Antarctic, while the Indian Ocean forms a connection in the east-west direction.

Very little was known about the bed of the ocean before it was decided to lay a submarine telegraph cable between Europe and America. Then, in order to carry out the work successfully, it was necessary to explore the ocean-floor.

This was done by **sounding**, that is, measuring the depth of water at a great number of places in the Atlantic.

The **sounding-line** is composed of steel wire, the end of which is carried to the bottom of the sea by means of sinkers—great masses of iron weighing about 100 lbs. As it would be very difficult to draw these up again, on account of the pressure exerted by the water, the apparatus is so constructed that they are detached on reaching the bottom. The length of line paid out before this occurs is recorded, and so the depth of the water is found.

Fig. 19. The British Isles (Bathy-orographical).

In addition a hollow rod, which forms the end of the sounding-line, brings up a sample of the sea-floor for examination.

Investigations of this kind have been carried out in all oceans in recent years ; in fact the work is almost constantly in progress, and fresh additions to our knowledge of the ocean are always being made.

The ocean floor is very uneven, though by no means so rugged as a land surface, because it is protected from the action of those forces which sculpture the rocks. In the Atlantic and the Pacific, it is generally from two to three miles below the surface. Much greater soundings than these have been obtained however. At a point not far from Porto Rico in the West Indies, the ocean is over five miles deep. The greatest known depth in the Pacific was discovered a short distance eastwards from the Ladrone Islands. It is nearly six miles. It is a curious fact that the deepest parts of the oceans are not near the middle of the trough, but close to land.

You will have made the discovery that sea-water has a saline flavour. This is because it contains in solution a number of mineral substances, chief of which is common salt.

It would be difficult to explain here how the sea got its salt, though you will easily understand from what you read in the chapters on " Rain " and " Rivers " that the amount of mineral matter in the sea is ever being increased.

You will remember that evaporation is constantly in progress at the surface of the ocean. By this process pure water passes into the atmosphere ;

In the Humber estuary, at high-water.

where evaporation proceeds most rapidly, e.g. in the tropics, surface water is most salt.

Now the water yielded to the air by the sea descends as rain, and finally returns to the sea in the form of rivers.

River-water is described as **fresh**, but we know that it contains mineral matter which has been dissolved from the land over which it flows. Thus, though the ocean has probably been salt from the beginning, it is always giving pure water to the atmosphere, and receiving it again enriched by the addition of mineral matter—including common salt.

Those parts of the ocean which receive large supplies of fresh water through rainfall, e.g. the Western Pacific, or by the melting of ice, e.g. the North Atlantic, or, like the Baltic Sea, from rivers, are of course less salt than the rest.

Another fact which is noted by everyone who goes to the seaside is that **high-water** and **low-water** occur twice daily.

Twice every day a tidal wave is carried from the open ocean into the shallow seas, and for a period of six hours, bays and estuaries are filling. River-mouths are converted into arms of the sea, and ocean-going vessels are able to reach towns situated on rivers some distance inland. During the next six hours the tide is receding, or **ebbing**.

By **wave** is meant the upward and downward movement, without any forward motion, the rise and fall being experienced by each portion of water in turn. You could send a wave along a piece of cord attached to a hook in the wall, by giving the other end a quick " up and down jerk." When the wave-movement is communicated to water which gradually becomes shallower, the surface layer gets in advance of the lower ones whose movement is interfered with by the bottom. The upper portion therefore falls forward, and a wave rushes up the beach.

The formation of the tidal wave in the ocean is a consequence of the attractive power of the moon

Wave rolling shorewards.

and the sun, but we shall not deal with that now. You may observe, however, that specially high tides are experienced on our shores, at **full moon** and **new moon**.

When it reaches the British Isles, the tidal wave is broken into several parts, one of which goes round the north of Ireland and Scotland, whilst another divides itself between the Irish Sea and the English

Channel. The northern and southern portions reach the Thames at the same time—a distinct advantage to the Port of London. Southampton has four tides a day ; for the wave which traverses the English Channel sends one branch up the Solent and, two hours later, a second one up Spithead. Seas which have a narrow connection with the ocean, the Mediterranean for example, are almost tideless.

Destructive action of the sea at Osgodby Nab, near Scarborough

On the other hand, a sea or estuary which has a wide entrance but narrows inland like a funnel, has very strong tides.

The Bristol Channel, for instance, is entered by the tidal wave which, being more and more compressed, gradually increases in height, and advances as a **bore**—a mass of water with a wall-like front nine feet high.

It is easy to understand that the great volume of tidal water brought against the land twice a day will exercise destructive action.

Soft rocks are worn away rapidly. Where beds of hard and soft rocks occur alternately, a succession of inlets may result. Sea-worn caves are formed at the base of cliffs, and as this action continues, blocks of overhanging rock break away and fall. In course

Flamborough Head.

of time these blocks are broken up and carried farther out. The smaller pieces are flung against each other every time the waves roll over them. They become rounded, yielding the seashore pebbles so familiar to us all. The particles broken off in the process are washed still farther out, and go to form the belt of sand which lies upon the beach.

When modern maps are compared with those

made a century or more ago, it is found that great changes in coast-line have occurred. In the south-east of Yorkshire in particular the sea has been very destructive, for during the last 50 years land has been removed at the rate of three yards per annum. Many towns and villages have disappeared from this part of the country. The site of Ravenspur, for example, the port where Henry IV landed in 1399, is now covered by the sea. But at Flamborough Head, where the chalk wolds reach the sea, there is an example of resistance to wave-action.

There is another movement of oceanic waters to which we must give some consideration, and a simple experiment will help us to understand it. Place some water in a large dish, and holding a pair of bellows almost horizontally, pump air on to the surface at one side.

A number of tiny pieces of wood sprinkled on the water will float along to the opposite end of the dish, whence dividing into two groups they will return along the sides. A current has been established in the water.

Let us now consider what is taking place in the Atlantic.

A certain belt of the ocean, south of the equator, is traversed by constant winds called the **South-East Trades**. They blow with remarkable persistency in the same direction, and so set up a current called the South Equatorial Drift. This travels in a somewhat westerly direction, and is divided into two parts by the wedge-shaped land of Brazil.

If we put a stone in our dish of water to project above the surface we can illustrate this.

One branch of the South Equatorial Drift flows southwards as the Brazilian Current, whilst the other takes a north-west course to the West Indies. Here a further division occurs, but the two parts are united later.

A large portion reaches the Gulf of Mexico, and, aided by the great volume of water from the Mississippi, forms there a reservoir, whose level is above that of the external ocean. Consequently a flow of water takes place through the Florida Strait, at the rate of about four miles per hour. This travels along the coast of North America, spreading out and decreasing in speed, under the name **Gulf Stream**.

Its volume is increased by the North Equatorial Drift, which is set up by the **North-East Trades**, on the north side of the equator. Coming from the tropics, the water of the Gulf Stream is warmer than that of the ocean it is traversing.

In the neighbourhood of Newfoundland, it is cut off—at any rate during part of the year—by the cold Labrador current whose origin we shall refer to immediately.

If the Gulf Stream makes any progress towards the open ocean, it can seldom be detected. Some distance to the east, however, another current is noted. It is the **North Atlantic Drift**, produced by the **Westerly Winds**. This current also divides when it approaches land, part flowing south as the Canaries Current, whilst the rest, the **European Current,** reaches the Arctic Ocean, and has some influence on the rate of melting of ice.

When the ice melts rapidly, a high level of water is established in the neighbourhood. A southward

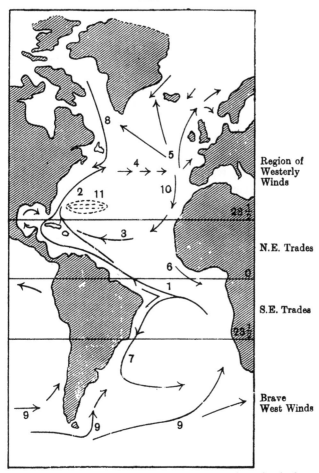

Fig. 20. The Directions of the chief Currents in the Atlantic Ocean.

1. S. Equatorial.	6. Guinea Counter Current.
2. Gulf Stream.	7. Brazilian.
3. N. Equatorial.	8. Labrador (cold).
4. North Atlantic Drift.	9. West Wind Drift (cold).
5. European and branches.	10. Canaries Current.

11. Sargasso Sea.

flow follows in the shape of the cold Labrador current.

This current will of course be stronger in the Spring and Summer than at other times. You will remember that we referred to the presence of icebergs in the North Atlantic, in the last chapter.

The currents already mentioned circulate about an area in the Atlantic which is comparatively at rest. It is not surprising that into this area there drifts seaweed, washed from the shores of the West Indies and America, and other floating material. It forms a **Sargasso Sea**, that is a seaweed sea.

In the South Atlantic there is an easterly drift, caused by the **Brave West Winds**, and a branch of this flows along the west coast of Africa, as the cold Benguela Current.

The circulation of water in the Pacific and Indian Oceans has a certain resemblance to that of the Atlantic, except that the change in direction of the Monsoons from north-east to south-west causes a reversal in direction of currents. Make a study of these currents, using your atlas-maps.

Currents affect the climate of lands beside which they flow, and particularly as regards rainfall.

The air over a warm current can hold much moisture ; and this, if carried over cool land, will be condensed, and fall as rain. This explains the heavy rainfall of the east coasts of Brazil, Africa and Australia.

On the other hand, since cool air has small capacity for moisture, south-west Africa, Peru, and Chile, against which cold currents flow, have a dry climate.

EXERCISES

1. Draw in rough outline the shore-lines of (a) the Atlantic, (b) the Pacific, (c) the Indian Oceans, and name the adjacent lands. Insert the equator and the tropics. Show the situation of the chief submarine ridges by means of a dotted line.

2. In your drawing of the Atlantic mark the position of Tristan da Cunha, St Helena, Ascension, the Azores, and Iceland; also the ridge which separates the Atlantic from the Arctic Ocean.

In the Pacific and Indian Oceans mark the position of the chief island groups.

3. On outline maps of the oceans, indicate the course of the chief currents by means of single lines, distinguishing warm and cold currents by thick and thin lines respectively, and show the direction by means of arrows.

4. Make drawings of inlets which the tide enters as a "bore," e.g., Bristol Channel, mouth of the Kent (Morecambe Bay), Bay of Fundy, The Hooghly (Ganges).

IX. LAKES

Movements of the earth's crust, to which we referred in a previous chapter, sometimes cause a portion of the sea to be entirely cut off by land from the main body of water. In this way an **inland sea** or **salt-water lake** is formed.

The Caspian Sea is a fine example. The existence of salt-marshes between this great lake and the Black Sea leads to the conclusion that the two were formerly connected ; and the Aral Sea, which lies further east, probably formed part of the same sheet of salt water.

The latter is diminishing in area, because it loses

by evaporation more water than rivers carry into it. For this reason also it is becoming more salt.

In the case of the Caspian, loss by evaporation is about balanced by the contribution of rivers.

We must not assume that all salt lakes have once been part of the sea. It is believed that the Dead Sea in Palestine, and the Great Salt Lake in North America, were once fresh-water lakes, and reached their present extremely salt condition through loss of water by evaporation.

Let us now perform a simple experiment. Dissolve half a teaspoonful of common salt in a quart of water. You will scarcely be able to detect the salt flavour of the solution. Transfer it to a pan, and bring it to boiling-point over a fire. Allow **boiling** to continue until the volume of the liquid is reduced to a pint. The saltness will now be very pronounced, and will become still more so if the volume is reduced further.

If the remainder be heated in a porcelain basin over a bunsen burner until all the water has evaporated, the salt will be recovered—it will be found deposited on the inside of the basin.

This experiment corresponds to what is taking place in salt lakes, such as the Dead Sea and the Great Salt Lake. The amount of water in them is diminishing—old shore-lines at higher levels than the present surface have been discovered.

In very dry seasons part of the bed of these lakes is exposed, showing a deposit of salt and other mineral matter.

The salt beds in Cheshire were formed by the drying up of a great salt lake which was in existence ages ago.

The number of salt lakes in the world is small.

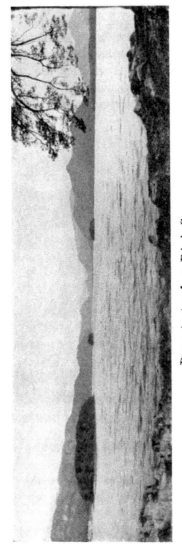

Derwentwater, from Friar's Crag.

The hills on the left are volcanic; those on the right are built of slate.

By far the greater number consist of fresh water, which is constantly being supplied by rivers. Hence they have an overflow, by which surplus water is carried to the sea. You have probably watched a tiny stream of rain-water flow from the middle of the street towards the side channel. The water will fill up a hollow in the pavement, and then overflowing

Red Tarn (altitude of surface 2356 ft.) and Striding Edge, Helvellyn.

at the lowest part of the surrounding edge, resume its course.

Very many lakes have been formed in an exactly similar manner, i.e. by the filling up of hollows in the surface of the earth by rivers.

Different forces have played a part in making these hollows or "lake-basins."

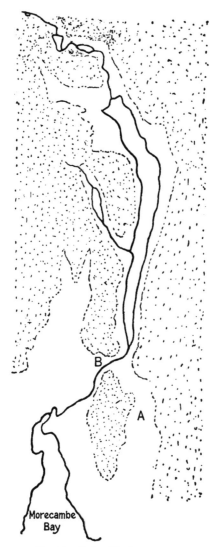

Fig. 21. Lake Windermere.

The small lakes to the north are Rydal Water and Grasmere; that to the west is Esthwaite Water.

The overflow from Windermere (River Leven) appears to have been diverted from valley *A* to *B*, by the deposit of boulder-clay.

Some, as you already know, are due to the carving and solvent action of rain and running water.

In our own islands, hundreds of small lakes and tarns lie in hollows formed by one of these processes. Most of them are too small to be well known, but you can find them on a large scale map. Malham Tarn, formed by the river Aire, is an example. In Cheshire, small shallow lakes called **meres** occupy

A Horse-shoe Bend which the river has practically abandoned. The main stream (Wharfe), seen in the background, is about 30 feet in width.

hollows formed by the sinking of the land, in places where solution of rock-salt has occurred underground.

Glaciers are responsible for the formation of many basins, by the removal of surface material, or by the irregular deposition of boulder-clay. In North Germany and in Finland thousands of hollows in the surface of glacial deposits are occupied by lakes.

Our own chief lake, Windermere, was formed—or at any rate its depth and area were increased—by the blocking up of the mouth of a valley with boulder-clay.

The Märjelen See in Switzerland is due to the glacier itself — the Great Aletsch Glacier—acting as a dam across the valley.

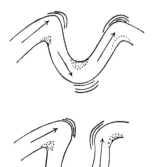

Another very interesting kind of lake is the **cut-off**, formed when a river cuts a new channel between two parts of a bend. This, by the way, is a case in which a river *straightens* its course. The Mississippi and the Australian Murray are specially noted for the formation of **cut-off** or **ox-bow** lakes.

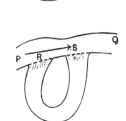

In Chapter II we noticed that lakes act as filters of river-water.

A small stream and a tiny lake show this action perfectly well, and you may even find an illustration for yourself on an uneven road after a shower of rain.

The sediment carried into a lake gradually fills up the basin. The coarser material is deposited where the river enters the lake, but the finer particles will be distributed further out, towards the middle.

Fig. 22. Stages in the formation of an "ox-bow" lake.

The arrows in the upper figures are directed towards points where the mechanical action of the water is greatest.

When the river has cut a direct channel between P and Q, the process of blocking up the ends of the horse-shoe bend, R and S, is carried on rapidly. (Refer to the preceding illustration.)

A delta is therefore built up at the head of the lake.

In Cumberland one large lake was actually divided into two smaller ones—Derwentwater and Bassenthwaite, by streams building out new land from opposite sides. These lakes are now separated by what is called an **alluvial flat**. When you go to Keswick you

A Delta.
(The pond is being slowly filled up.)

must climb Latrigg, a hill which really forms part of the Skiddaw mass. From its summit you will have a splendid view of the two lakes and the flat land between them. The lakes are now connected by the river Derwent.

In course of time the overflow from a lake will cut its channel so deeply that all the water in the lake will drain off. The sediment deposited by the inflowing river will of course help to bring about this result.

The Vale of Pickering is an excellent illustration. If you examine the map you will notice a tract of almost level land lying between the Yorkshire Wolds and the North York Moors.

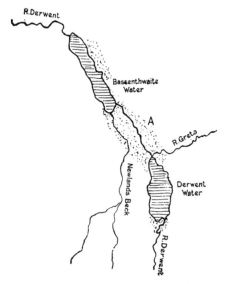

Fig. 23. The dotted area *A* is the alluvial flat formed by Newlands Beck and the Greta.

It is traversed by the river Derwent (the Yorkshire Derwent) which, at the town of Malton, enters and flows through a narrow gap of its own construction.

The Vale of Pickering was occupied by a lake during the Great Ice Age, and the water was drained off through the gorge just mentioned.

Lakes add greatly to the beauty of a landscape.
The English Lake District is one of the prettiest
parts of the country, and is visited by great numbers
of people during the holiday season.

During recent years, however, a problem for the
people of great cities to solve has been how to obtain

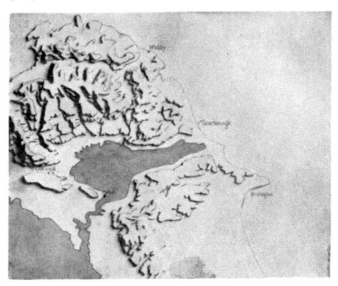

Fig. 24. The Vale of Pickering.
(Photograph of Relief-map.)

good supplies of drinking-water. In many cases the
problem has been solved by making use of lakes.

Thirlmere in Cumberland, for example, is the
source of Manchester's supply. The water is carried
along a pipe-track 96 miles long, through pipes three
to four feet in diameter. Liverpool obtains water
from Lake Vyrnwy in Wales by means of an aqueduct
which is 66 miles long.

The beautiful Loch Katrine, in Perthshire, is the main source of drinking-water for Glasgow. But the

Ullswater—one of the most beautiful of English lakes.

requirements of this city are increasing so rapidly that additional sources are being looked for, and probably other lakes will be drawn upon.

We must not close this chapter without a reference to the greatest lakes in the world. They are in America, and are frequently named the Great Lakes. Superior itself is almost as large as Ireland, and the area of the five : Superior, Huron, Michigan, Erie and Ontario is over 90,000 square miles ; or 6000 square miles greater than the area of Great Britain.

They form a very valuable means of communication for Canada and the United States.

The Niagara Falls lie between Erie and Ontario, but the Welland Canal enables vessels to pass from one lake to the other.

Two other canals, the Canadian and the American, have been cut, so that vessels may avoid the rapids of the St Mary River, which connects Lake Superior to Lake Huron.

Wheat-lands, maize-lands and forested areas lie in the neighbourhood of the Great Lakes, and there are valuable stores of iron and copper ore near Lake Superior. You will therefore not be surprised to learn that the traffic across the lakes is in ore, grain and flour, timber, and coal ; but it may astonish you to hear that the annual tonnage of Cleveland on Lake Erie is equal to that of Liverpool.

EXERCISES

1. Make two diagrams, one a plan (looking from above) and the other a section, showing how sediment is deposited by a river on entering a lake.

2. Draw a map of the English Lake District, and shade the high land. Describe the arrangement of the lakes. Mark the position of the chief towns and their railway connections with other parts of the country.

3. Make sketches of Lake Chad (Africa) and Lake Eyre

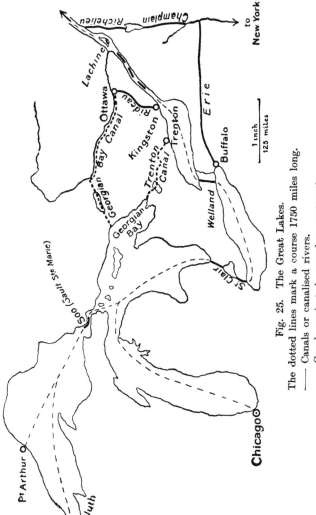

Fig. 25. The Great Lakes.

The dotted lines mark a course 1750 miles long.

—— Canals or canalised rivers.

...... Canals projected or under construction.

(Australia) and their feeders. Why have these lakes no overflow to the sea ? Find other lakes of the same type in Asia and America.

4. Windermere is ten miles long, and its maximum depth is 220 feet. Assume the lake to be 220 feet deep in every part and try to make a scale-drawing of its basin.

X. ISLANDS

In the last chapter we saw that one consequence of movement of the earth's crust is the formation of inland seas.   Such a result is due to an uplift.

Fig. 26. Submerged England (South).

We must now consider the consequences of some downward movements.

First, suppose the British Isles to be depressed through 500 feet.

The sea would flood a great part of the country, whilst all land having an altitude of over 500 feet would project above the water.

The Chilterns, the Cotswolds and the Downs would become chains of islands (Fig. 26).

The Pennines would yield several large islands, with a number of smaller ones near them, and eastwards would lie detached islands, the remnants of the Wolds and the Cleveland Hills (Fig. 27).

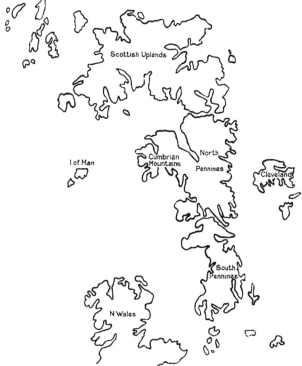

Fig. 27. Submerged England (North).

If you examine a physical map, you will be able to pick out other islands. You might even make a drawing to show the new British archipelago, or, what is even better, make for yourself in a shallow dish a rough model in plasticine of part of England.

The northern counties would be very suitable, because they include lowlands and highlands in a comparatively small area.

Pour into the dish sufficient water to flood, say, the Vale of Pickering.

No further explanation will be required to make it clear that if the sea floods a land area, the high parts, remaining unsubmerged, become islands.

This is exactly what is supposed to have happened to the western part of Europe, long ago.

An East Coast Promontory. (Saltwick.)
The extremity is an island at high-water only.

The British Isles are the high parts of a region which was flooded by the sea, either through the sinking of the land, or by the rising of the sea-level. The North Sea, the English Channel and other British seas lie in what were the valleys and low-lying tracts of this region.

You will certainly wish to know what led to this supposition.

You must refer to a map showing the depth of the North Sea. You will notice that between England and Denmark it is in most places not more than 180 feet deep, whilst part of the Dogger Bank is within 60 feet of the surface.

It is the shallowness of the North Sea, together with the fact that bones of land animals have been dredged up from the Dogger Bank, that led people to suppose that Britain and the surrounding seas at one time formed part of the continent. The idea is supported by the similarity of the rocks on opposite sides of the Channel. The chalk Downs of Kent and

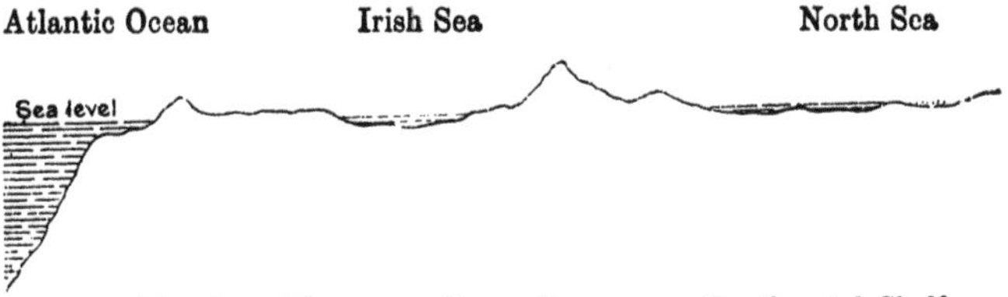

Fig. 28. Diagrammatic section across Continental Shelf.

Sussex, for instance, have a continental extension in the chalk hills of North France.

Because of their mode of origin, the British Isles are described as **Continental Islands** ; and the sub-merged portion of the continent, which, as we noted in Chapter VIII, extends about 200 miles beyond Ireland, is called the **Continental Shelf**.

The British Isles are the unsubmerged part of the continental shelf.

There are many other interesting examples. Look at the long chain of Frisian Islands, lying near the coasts of Holland and Germany ; and the islands off the Scandinavian coast. Sometimes it is possible to trace a mountain system from the mainland through a chain of islands. The Sierra Nevada mountains in Spain, for example, reappear in the Balearic Islands.

Continental islands are to be found along the shores of all the continents.

A great number are arranged in festoons along the western side of the Pacific Ocean. The East Indies include islands some of which formed part of Asia, whilst others belonged to Australia.

But you will find marked on your map islands such as St Helena and Ascension in the South Atlantic, or the Sandwich group in the Pacific, which are far away from the great land masses, and separated from them by deep water. This indicates that they have no connection with the continents.

They are in the midst of the ocean, and are classed as **Oceanic Islands**.

Many are composed of igneous rock, and have been built up by volcanoes which burst forth on the ocean floor.

You will see, then, that such islands must be the summits of mountains. But we must use the term **summit** with caution, for Teneriffe in the Canary Group towers 12,000 feet above the sea, and many of the Pacific islands have mountains 4000 feet high.

St Helena in the Atlantic, and St Paul in the Indian Ocean are solitary volcanic peaks ; but oceanic islands frequently occur in groups, and often rise from a submarine ridge.

Ascension and Tristan da Cunha rise from a ridge which divides the bed of the South Atlantic into two portions, and the Azores stand on a ridge in the North Atlantic.

On the floor of the Pacific a number of ridges are

known, and they form the foundations of such groups as the Sandwich, and the Society Islands.

There is a second type of oceanic island, which differs from those mentioned above in almost every respect. It is composed of limestone ; it rises very little above the surface of the water ; and it is the work of tiny creatures—the coral polyps, which live crowded together in great colonies. These coral animals have a hard skeleton, composed of carbonate of lime, a substance they are able to extract from sea-water.

When they die, the skeletons remain. So numerous are they, that they form great reefs of limestone. Corals die when they are exposed to air, so the structure cannot be carried above the surface. But particles and fragments of coral rock are broken off by the force of the waves and flung on to the top of the reef.

This debris, with the addition of other matter floated on to the reef by the sea, forms a soil which, in time, will support vegetation. Corals can only live in water which is shallow, clear and warm. Their reefs must therefore be built not far from land, but away from the mouths of rivers, and in warm seas.

Many exist in the West Indies region, in the Indian Ocean—in fact in all tropical seas ; but the greatest of coral structures is the Great Barrier Reef, which lies off the north-east coast of Australia. It is over a thousand miles long, and the channel which separates it from the shore is from ten to thirty miles wide.

But, as we have already said, there are *oceanic* coral islands ; and many attempts have been made to explain how shallow-water creatures could build islands in the middle of the ocean.

They are circular in form, and are called **atolls**.

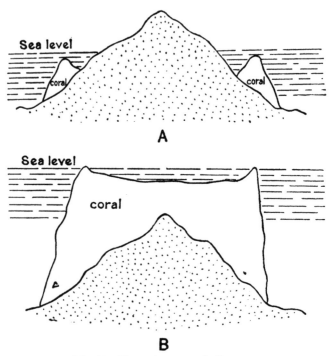

Fig. 29. Formation of an Atoll.

Reef-builders begin their work in shallow water near the shores of an island (*A*), and if the island is part of a sinking area, the coral structure will eventually cover the submerged island (*B*). If no sinking occurs, the coral rock will be built up to the surface of the water and form a *fringing reef* around the island.

The enclosed lagoons of sea-water have a connection, by means of a gap in the ring of low land, with the outer ocean. Because of their shape, it was at one time believed that these islands were built on the rims of submarine craters.

It is now thought, however, that the corals built their reefs in shallow water as usual, but around islands.

Movements of the earth's crust must have caused the islands to sink beneath the surface of the sea. But the reef-builders continued their work, and, as

South Sea Island Plantation.

they managed to raise the structure to the surface, the rate of building must have been about equal to the rate at which the islands sank. Evidently the downward movement of the ocean bed was very slow indeed.

If you examine a map of the South Seas, i.e. the South Pacific Ocean, you will see how great is the number of oceanic islands.

They occur in groups : the Solomons, the Carolines, the New Hebrides, and the Fiji Islands. All of these are partly volcanic, with lofty peaks, and partly coral, whilst the Low Archipelago consists of about 80 little coral islands.

During recent years the importance of the South Sea Islands to the commercial world has greatly increased, because of their coconut plantations.

The dried flesh of the coconut, known as **copra,** is exported in large quantities for the sake of the coconut-oil it contains. Coconut-oil has long been used by makers of soap, but lately it has been in great demand for the manufacture of margarine.

Consequently the price of copra has become much higher, and greater attention has been paid to the South Sea plantations.

The volcanic islands possess a very fertile soil, which produces rich fruits and crops with little labour, and the inhabitants are lazy. On the coral islands life is much harder. The people must work for their living, and many are occupied in the copra trade.

We will conclude this chapter with Robert Louis Stevenson's fine description of the South Sea Islands.

"That wide field of ocean, called loosely the South Seas, extends from tropic to tropic....Much of it lies vacant ; much is closely sown with isles, and the isles are of two sorts. No distinction is so continually dwelt upon in South Sea talk as that between ' low ' and ' high ' islands and there is none more broadly marked in nature....On the one hand, and chiefly in groups of from eight to a dozen, volcanic islands rise above the sea; few reach an altitude of less than 4000 feet; one exceeds 13,000; their tops

are often obscured in cloud ; they are all clothed
with various forests, all abound in food, and are all
remarkable for picturesque and solemn scenery. On
the other hand we have the atoll ;...rudely annular
in shape ; enclosing a lagoon ; rarely extending
beyond a quarter of a mile at its chief width ; often
rising at its highest point to less than the stature of
a man—man himself, the rat, and the land-crab, its
chief inhabitants ; not more variously supplied with
plants ; and offering to the eye, even when perfect,
only a rim of glittering beach and verdant foliage,
enclosing and enclosed by the blue sea."

EXERCISES

1. Explain the difference between an "insular" and a
"continental" climate.

2. Give an explanation of the presence of islands in some
of our English lakes, e.g., Windermere and Derwentwater.

3. Refer to the maps of Europe, Asia and America, and
make drawings of continental islands. Include the adjacent
shore-line of the continent in each case.

4. Make a diagrammatic section showing the edge of
a continent, continental islands, ocean bed and oceanic islands.

5. In the East Indies, some of the islands have animal
and vegetable life like those of Asia, whilst others possess
Australian features. Write a short explanation.

XI. VEGETATION AND ANIMAL LIFE

In this chapter we shall consider the vegetation
which clothes the surface of the earth, and make some
reference also to animal life.

As you know from observation in gardens and
greenhouses, moisture and heat favour the growth

of plants. Vegetation is therefore most luxuriant in those parts of **the torrid zone** that have a plentiful supply of rain.

In the neighbourhood of the equator, in the basins of the Amazon and the Congo, in the Malay Peninsula and the adjacent islands rainfall is very heavy, and the plant life of those regions is the finest in the world.

A clearing in the Tropical Forest, Malay Peninsula.

Trees are remarkable for their height, but not less so for their girth. Massive trunks rise without a branch to a height of 150 feet, and then throw out branches and foliage so thickly as to prevent sunlight from getting through.

Beneath these are lesser trees which flourish in the shade.

Wonderful climbing plants are seen everywhere. They twine around the stems of trees, making their way up to light, or twist along the branches, linking one tree to another.

The ground is covered with a thick undergrowth of tree-ferns, climbing ferns, fungi and other plants, matted together by creepers in such a tangled mass that it is difficult to say to which tree or plant the leaves, flowers and fruit really belong.

Wallace, in his *Travels on the Amazon and Rio Negro*, describes an extraordinary plant which not only grows as a " good-sized tree out of the ground, but is also parasitical on almost every other forest tree. Its large whitish fruits," he continues, " are called ' wild onion ' by the natives and are much eaten by birds, which probably carry seeds into the forks of lofty trees, where it seems most readily to take root in any little decaying vegetable matter which may be there ; and when it arrives at such a size as to require more nourishment than it can there obtain, it sends down long shoots to the ground, which take root and grow into a new stem."

Animals are to a great extent crowded out by plants. But the alligator haunts the rivers of the Brazilian forest, and the jaguar has its home on their banks. The trees are peopled with monkeys, birds, and snakes, and everywhere is heard the hum of myriads of insects.

Kingsley, in *Westward Ho!*, gives an interesting picture of a forest scene. " As the sun rose higher and higher, a great stillness fell upon the forest. The jaguars and the monkeys had hidden themselves in the darkest depths of the woods ; the birds' notes

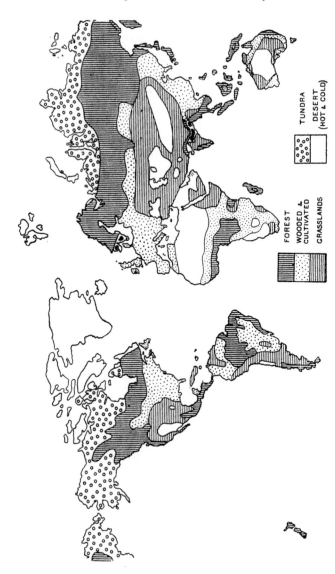

Fig. 30. The World's Vegetation Regions.
(In broad outline, and irrespective of modifications due to mountain systems.)

died out one by one ; the very butterflies ceased their flitting over the tree-tops, and slept with outspread wings upon the glossy leaves, undistinguishable from the flowers around them. Now and then a colibri (humming-bird) whirred downward toward the water, hummed for a moment around some pendent flower, and then the living gem was lost in the deep blackness of the inner wood, amongst tree-trunks as huge and dark as the pillars of some Hindoo shrine ; or a parrot swung and screamed from an overhanging bough ; or a thirsty monkey slid lazily down a liana to the surface of the stream, dipped up the water in his tiny hand, and started chattering back, as his eyes met those of some foul alligator peering upward through the clear depths below.''

The equatorial forests yield many products of great value, such as timber used in cabinet-making— mahogany, rosewood and ebony; rubber, palm oil, ground nuts, coconuts, sago and quinine.

Where the land has been cleared, great numbers of rubber trees have been planted; and sugar, bananas and coffee are cultivated. These, and many other plants such as the cacao or cocoa tree, tea, rice, and cotton can only be grown successfully in hot regions where rain is abundant. Of this group, however, the tea-shrub is the hardiest. It can endure frost and has therefore a rather wide climatic range.

In **the temperate zones,** rainfall is neither so heavy nor so regular, and vegetation is not so dense as within the tropics.

In regions like the Mediterranean, where the summer is warm and dry, and the winter cool and moist, the evergreen forest flourishes. It consists of such trees as the myrtle, olive, cork-oak, holly.

In New Zealand, which lies in about the same latitude south as the Mediterranean region does in the north, there is a rich evergreen vegetation. The kauri pine is conspicuous, with a trunk eight or ten feet thick. Lianas and flowering creepers are common ; but one of the most beautiful characteristic plants is the tree-fern. It often grows to a height of 60 feet, and gives a somewhat tropical appearance to the vegetation. The chief trees in the Australian forests belong to the eucalyptus species ; one of them, the jarrah, provides timber for paving streets. In the cooler parts of the temperate zone, the oak, elm, ash, and beech are typical trees. They are deciduous, i.e. they shed their leaves in the autumn. This is the kind of vegetation which occurs naturally over a great part of Central Europe, and, as you know, in our own land. In England, however, the natural forest was cleared long ago. The woodlands of to-day are of comparatively recent formation.

Where the climate is cooler still, with short summers, severe winters and rather deficient rainfall, the trees are of the coniferous variety—the pine, fir and larch.

The coniferous forest clothes a large part of northern Canada, northern Europe, especially Scandinavia and Russia, and Siberia. But we must remember that both coniferous and deciduous forests grow on high mountains within the tropics; for the slopes of a snow-capped peak in a hot land show those changes of climate which are experienced in travelling from the tropics to the Arctic regions.

A New Zealand recreation-ground.
Showing tree-ferns, which are so characteristic of New Zealand vegetation.

From the temperate forests have been obtained huge quantities of timber for use in building, mining, the construction of ships, and almost every other industry.

Though great tracts of land have been cleared and devoted to the raising of crops, the work of **lumbering** is still very important in Canada and the Baltic countries.

In the Coniferous Forest Belt, Canada.

The demand for timber for ship-building diminished when iron came into use for the purpose; but the use of wood-pulp in the manufacture of paper, picture-frames and many other articles, makes timber as important in commerce to-day as ever it was.

Rivers have special value in lumbering areas. They provide an easy and cheap means of transport for logs, and waterfalls supply power for working saw-mills and pulp-mills.

The warmer parts of the temperate zone are great fruit-producing areas. The vine occupies an important place. It is cultivated in Mediterranean lands, and others which have a similar climate. It is grown, for example, in California and Chile ; and in South Africa, South Australia and New Zealand, cultivation of the vine is becoming a very important occupation.

Gathering Grapes, New Zealand Fruit-farm.

Other fruits which love a warm climate are the fig, orange, lemon, pomegranate, all of which are exported from the Mediterranean region.

Further north, in countries whose climate resembles that of England, there are fruit trees of more hardy nature. Apples, pears and stone fruits flourish.

We may here notice, too, that Australia is now able to send great quantities of apples to England.

As the Australians have summer during our winter, the fruit is ready for export when English and American supplies are exhausted.

Animal life is as abundant in the cool forest as it is scarce in the hot equatorial forest, though it has been greatly reduced by hunting, for the sake of furs and skins, and by clearing the land for agricultural purposes. The bear, wolf and boar are the chief wild animals in the Old World ; the grizzly bear, lynx and beaver are typical forms in the New World temperate region.

In all the areas mentioned above, the forest thins towards the parts where rainfall is scanty, and finally gives place to **grass-land.**

The llanos, north of the Amazon basin, the prairies of North America, the pampas of South America, the steppes of Russia, and the extensive grass-lands of central and southern Africa are regions where the rainfall is insufficient for heavy vegetation, and the land is covered with grass.

New Zealand provides a striking illustration of the relation between rainfall and vegetation. The western portion of the islands receives abundant rain from the west winds, and was until recently clothed with dense forests—much has been cut down. The eastern portion is much drier, and consists of grass-covered plains.

The grass-lands of the world have always been pasture-lands for animals, the chief drawback being the scarcity of water. Some of them are still inhabited by nomadic peoples, who dwell in a particular area only so long as it yields food and water for their cattle.

Originally they were inhabited by herds of bison, deer, horses or other creatures having the power of rapid movement—an aid in escaping from beasts of prey like the lion, tiger and hyena, which make their home near a supply of flesh food.

Savanna is the name given to natural park-land, i.e. grass-land with scattered trees within the tropics. This is the ideal home for those creatures described as **big game,** including, in addition to those named in the preceding paragraph, the elephant, giraffe, zebra and rhinoceros.

In Australia are found animals of a peculiar type called marsupials, that is, pouched animals. Chief of these is the kangaroo.

At the present day great herds of cattle and flocks of sheep are reared on the world's grass-lands. South America and New Zealand have become important as sources for supply of flesh food. The frozen meat exported from these places has a prominent place in English markets.

It is from Australia, New Zealand, South Africa, and other pasture-lands that we obtain our chief supplies of wool. In some places—the American prairies and part of the Argentine, great changes have taken place. They are excellent wheat-growing regions, and the natural grasses have been replaced by those cultivated for human food. Farms are very extensive, and all kinds of labour-saving machinery are employed to work them. Maize also is grown.

Over some parts of the earth's surface rainfall is so slight that not even grass will grow. Such are the Sahara, the **deserts** of Asia and North America, the Atacama desert in South America, the Kalahari of

South Africa and the Great Australian desert. They are situated, some in the north, some in the south, near one of the **tropics,** except those of Central Asia.

The temperature on summer days is very high, for the sun's rays strike almost vertically. During the night, the land cools rapidly, partly in consequence of the absence of vegetation.

These great and frequent changes of temperature cause the rocks to break up. Winds carry on the

Canadian Wheat-land.

In 1925, Canada produced over four hundred and sixteen million bushels of wheat, and five hundred million bushels of oats.

work of destruction, blowing fragments against each other, breaking them into particles, which, becoming rounded by friction, form the sand described as "desert-sand." In describing a journey through the Libyan desert, Dr MacDougal says, "A distance of forty miles of gravel, sand and broken rock was traversed, in which no vestige of any kind of plant dead or alive was found.... We suffered from cold during the night though clothed as if for an arctic climate."

But a desert is not merely a sandy waste, nor is it level land. High mountains cross the Sahara, and in winter they are often capped with snow.

All deserts have an inland drainage system, consisting of streams which either lose themselves in the sand, or flow into a depression and so form a marsh or lake.

In the Sahara there are many oases, where date-palms and other plants flourish. The water, supplied by springs, must have found its way from some distant region, perhaps on the borders of the desert, by an underground route.

Tafilet is one of many large oases. It has a considerable population, and exports large quantities of dates, some of which reach the English markets.

The vegetation of the desert proper belongs to the gum-acacia and cactus families—plants specially suited, by their water-storing qualities, to regions where rain falls in small quantities and at long intervals. Their thick fleshy stems, having spines instead of leaves, lose little by evaporation.

There are two other great barren regions on the surface of the earth. They are **the cold deserts** which lie around the poles of the earth.

Much of the land is never free from its covering of ice. The low temperature, and terrible blizzards which frequently sweep over these regions, make life in any form almost impossible.

In spite of this numerous expeditions have visited both the Arctic and Antarctic regions, for the purpose

The "Dancing Bear," Brimham, near Harrogate.

A block of sandstone fantastically carved by those agents which break up the rocks of desert areas; viz. great variations in temperature, and wind-driven dust. On English moorlands, hot summer days are usually succeeded by very cool nights.

of exploration, or to achieve the distinction of reaching **the Pole.**

In the year 1909, an American explorer, Lieut. Peary, succeeded in penetrating the Arctic regions to the north pole. Expeditions in the Antarctic then made a strenuous effort to reach the south pole, eventually with success. Captain Scott reached it in

Seals basking on "pancake" ice-floes. (Off Cape Evans.)
(From a copyright photograph by H. G. Ponting, F.R.G.S.)

January, 1912, only to find that Capt. Amundsen, a Norwegian, had been there a little earlier.

The return journey of Scott's polar party was made extremely difficult by unusually severe climatic conditions, and at last, unable to advance further because of a furious blizzard which raged for over a week,

Scott and his companions died from exposure and want of food, " in that silent wilderness of snow."

Perhaps the most remarkable discovery made by explorers in the polar regions is the abundance of fossilised vegetation in the sedimentary rocks. This proves that these icebound regions must once have enjoyed a warm climate.

In the north of Siberia, the north-east of Europe

Yorkshire Moorland.

and in northern Canada there are tracts of land where the deeper layers are always frozen. But during the short summer the surface is softened by the sun's rays, and then the **Tundras** are converted into swamps.

The characteristic vegetation of the tundra consists of mosses and lichens, the chief food of the reindeer, and stunted shrubs which under more favourable conditions would develop into trees. In the summer, however, other plants spring up, and even reach the flowering stage. They resemble plants which grow on the mountains in warmer climates.

The summer vegetation of the dry parts of the tundra has in fact a counterpart in the bleak British moorlands, whose climate, though less extreme than that of the tundras, has a much greater range than that of the lowlands. The higher parts of the Pennines and Cumbrian mountains, and the Highlands of Scotland, will support little but heather and coarse grass, with occasionally a few hardy trees, which grow in sheltered hollows.

Southwards the tundra passes into the coniferous forest zone.

The polar bear, the arctic fox and arctic hare inhabit these northerly lands. But even these dreary lands are not without human inhabitants. Settled life is not possible, for vegetation is so scanty that domestic animals, of which the reindeer is chief, must move from one area to another to obtain supplies of food.

The people must obtain food by hunting and fishing ; though the short summer will enable them to obtain some vegetable food.

In the Antarctic regions, life-forms are more scarce than in the far north ; but the penguin is a curious, highly interesting bird.

The ocean contains countless forms of both vegetable and animal life, whose distribution depends upon the warmth and depth of the water. Light is essential to most life-forms, and as the sun's rays cannot penetrate the water much below 600 feet, the fauna of the dark, cold, deep water consists of peculiar sightless creatures, whose bodies are specially adapted to withstand tremendous pressure.

It is in shallow seas that seaweeds and animals are most numerous. Consequently the sea surrounding the continental land masses is rich in plant and animal life. The North Sea is an ideal region—it is one of the best fishing-grounds known. Cod, herring, plaice, whiting, halibut, ling are abundant. Across the Atlantic, in about the same latitude as the North Sea, lies another great fishing-ground—the Banks of Newfoundland. This is the most important cod-fishing area in the world. There are valuable fishing-grounds off the coasts of Japan.

Various kinds of "shell-fish," the oyster, crab, lobster, live near the land in temperate regions. In the warmer waters of the Mediterranean typical fish are the tunny, anchovy and sardine.

Sponges, which are found in many regions, flourish best in warm waters. They are dredged in the Mediterranean, Gulf of Mexico and Red Sea. In the Red Sea also, and in many places in the warm Indian Ocean, the pearl-oyster is found.

Fish which live in tropical seas are frequently brilliant in colouring, but seldom good for eating.

The cold polar regions have a distinctive sea fauna, the chief members of which are the seal and the whale, creatures which are hunted for the sake of the important commercial commodities they yield—seal skins, whalebone and oil. They are not fishes.

The Antarctic killer whale must be as formidable as the shark which lives in warm seas. Capt. Scott described the killer's array of teeth as by "far the largest and most terrifying in the world"; and he recorded an exciting adventure with six or seven killers, experienced by Mr Ponting, who was endeavouring to photograph them.

EXERCISES

1. Name regions where "natural" vegetation is still in existence, and areas where clearing has been carried out on a large scale.

2. Explain how the seeds which gave rise to vegetation on coral islands may have been conveyed thither.

3. Sometimes an abrupt change in the character of the vegetation is noticed in an area where the same climatic conditions prevail. Give an explanation, and refer to your own district for illustrations if possible.

4. The "Game Laws" of a portion of the British Empire relate to the following animals: Lion, cheetah, elephant, rhinoceros, giraffe, hippopotamus, zebra, antelope, gazelle, buffalo and others. Try to name this region, and give a short description of its vegetation.

XII.   HUMAN SETTLEMENTS

Whereabouts upon the surface of the earth the first men lived is not definitely known, but it is generally supposed to have been some part of Central Asia. From that region people must gradually have spread over the world, crossing to America and Australia by "land-bridges" that are now partly submerged.

The earliest human inhabitants of whom anything is known was the Stone Age man. Evidence of his existence has been found in river gravels and caves. Sometimes bones are discovered, but the chief relics of prehistoric man are the implements he used. These are of flint or other hard stone; the stone-man gave them an edge by chipping off fragments.

For thousands of years the Stone Age people would be hardly superior to the beasts against which they had to struggle for existence. Their food consisted of what nature provided—fruit and nuts, varied with flesh food as their skill in hunting developed. In the course of time they learned how to produce fire. This was followed by the use of metals, and so man passed out of the Stone Age.

Before that happened, however, people had begun to select areas for agricultural settlements. This was the beginning of a movement that continued through the Bronze Age into the Iron Age, and reached its highest development in modern times.

Man did not begin actually to write history until about eight or nine thousand years ago; consequently we do not possess complete knowledge of the beginnings of agriculture.

The earliest human settlements of which anything is definitely known, were established on the banks of the Nile and the Euphrates. By irrigating their land, the Egyptians and Babylonians made it produce an ample supply of food. Secure in this respect, they lived a settled life, amassed treasure, and devoted attention to the arts of civilisation. Their enemies were the nomadic tribes who lived on the open grasslands of the Old World, and who, driven by hunger or love of fighting and plunder, made frequent raids upon the settled peoples.

From these grasslands, however, people were continually migrating westwards. Some found a home on the steppes of Central Europe, some on the edge of the northern forests, and many on the shorelands and islands of the Mediterranean Sea. For several reasons the latter region became the world's centre of civilisation; its climate was very favourable to human life; it had many tracts of land very suitable for agriculture; its seas and gulfs encouraged trade between various groups of people; and its frontiers of mountains and deserts were a barrier against barbarian attacks.

The ancient Mediterranean peoples made such progress that the effects of their work have lasted even to the present day. The Phoenicians, who inhabited a narrow strip of country at the eastern end of the "Great Sea," became famous navigators; they traded with all known lands. Following close upon them were the famous "sea-kings" of Crete. Then came the Greeks who also engaged in foreign trade, but they distinguished themselves particularly in science, literature, and art. Both the Greeks and the Phoenicians established colonies at many points on the shores of the Mediterranean; one of the most famous Phoenician colonies was Carthage on the north coast of Africa.

The Romans played a most important part in the spread of civilisation. Their empire extended from Spain to Mesopotamia, and from the Sahara to Britain. They constructed good roads and buildings, caused the people to till the soil, and by strong wise government maintained peace within their borders.

But Roman power declined in the 5th century. You may read in history books how the empire broke up; how the Saxons, Angles and Danes fell upon Britain;

how the Vandals and Goths attacked Gaul and Spain, and even sacked the city of Rome; how the Franks drove the Goths south of the Pyrenees; how the Lombards seized northern Italy, and the Magyar horsemen took Hungary; how the Saracens swept through northern Africa, conquered Spain and advanced into the land of the Franks, to have their victorious career stopped in a terrible battle at Tours (732).

The final results of the events mentioned above were, that the number of settled people in Europe was greatly increased, and various groups became more or less united as nations. There followed an era—the Middle Ages—during which Europeans developed their industries and commerce, awaiting the call from the empty places of the world to another period of settlement making. The call came with the discovery of new lands in the 15th and 16th centuries, but before dealing with that we must refer briefly to the East.

Civilisation in India had its beginnings several thousand years ago, when a horde of people entered the country by the passes in the north-west. They overpowered the dark-skinned people who were already in possession, and established settlements in the basins of the Indus and the Ganges. In the course of time they extended their influence over the whole peninsula.

The conquerors came from the highlands of Asia— perhaps from Persia. They belonged originally to the same section of the white race as the Germanic tribes that played a part in breaking up the Roman empire; but living under different conditions, they gradually developed into a people of very different type. As the articles they produced were always in demand in Europe, there was a great deal of caravan traffic across the deserts that separate India from the Mediterranean.

Civilising influences were at work in the Far East at an even earlier period. Settlements were formed in the great valleys and plains of China, at least forty-five centuries ago. These, like the western colonies, appear to have suffered much in ancient days from nomadic raids.

A striking memorial of these troublous times is the Great Wall of China, built over 2000 years ago. The wall, constructed of brick, stone and earth, was carried for 1400 miles across valleys and over mountains, along the northern boundary of the country; it was intended as a defence against Mongolian attacks. Doubtless the wall was of considerable value, but it did not prevent the nomads from raiding China again and again.

Communication between the east and west of Eurasia was rendered difficult by huge mountains and deserts, and perhaps most of all by the presence of fierce nomadic tribes in the interior of Asia. Thus the Chinese and Japanese gained nothing from the wonderful achievements of the Arabs, Greeks and Romans, and they knew nothing of western discoveries until quite recent times. During the last fifty years the Japanese have endeavoured to learn everything that Europeans and Americans could teach them, and the Chinese are following the example of the Japanese.

We must now resume the story of European activities. In 1492, Columbus took his small vessels out into the unknown Atlantic, seeking to reach India by sailing westwards. What he actually did was to discover a New World.

The American continents were found to have a small

population, consisting mainly of nomads; but in Mexico and Peru there were peoples who had made considerable progress in civilisation. Europeans soon began to form settlements on the banks of rivers near the Atlantic coast. They cleared forest, cultivated the land, and began to trade with both the "Indians" and the mother-countries.

Gradually the white settlements spread towards the interior, giving rise eventually to English-speaking nations in Canada and the United States, and to nations largely of Spanish or Portuguese origin in Mexico, and in Central and South America.

There are, however, many "coloured people" in the Americas. The yellow race is represented by the Indians of whom there are considerable numbers in both continents, and by Chinese and Japanese, who have settled on the western shorelands of North America in recent times. The black race is represented by some ten million people in the United States; they are the descendants of those who were taken from Africa to work as slaves on the American plantations. More black people are settled in the West Indies and in South America.

The Cape route to India was discovered by Vasco da Gama in 1497, but for a long time South Africa was regarded as an inconvenient land area—lengthening the voyage to the East. Before the end of the 17th century, the Dutch established a settlement at Cape Town, which port they made a calling-place for their East Indiamen. The Dutch were followed by other Europeans, mainly British, and settlements gradually spread eastwards and northwards.

As in the case of some other colonies, gold mining

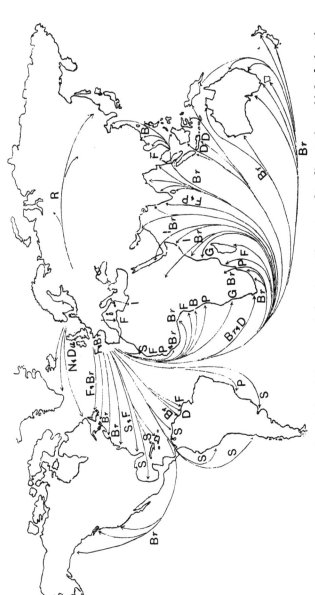

Fig. 31. Diagram illustrating the activity of Europeans in forming settlements and trading stations, chiefly during the 16th, 17th, 18th and 19th centuries. Many of the settlements have developed into nations, as described in this chapter, and some of these have severed the connection with the mother-country; a few stations and colonies have been transferred by treaty.

[Br = British; B = Belgian; D = Dutch; Da = Danish; F = French; G = German; I = Italian; N = Norse; P = Portuguese; R = Russian; S = Spanish.]

attracted many people. Gold was discovered on Witwatersrand in 1887, and the mining camp established there became the town of Johannesburg, with 100,000 inhabitants within ten years; its population is now 380,000 (1935).

A number of these African settlements—the Cape of Good Hope province, Natal, Transvaal, Orange Free State, Southern Rhodesia, and South-west Protectorate —now form the Union of South Africa, with an area about eight times that of the British Isles. Europeans form less than 25 per cent. of the population; the rest are blacks (Kaffirs, Hottentots, Bechuanas, etc.) or Asiatics (Hindus, Malays, etc.).

The African natives have benefited by contact with European civilisation. They have their own reserves, where they can possess land. Many, however, live amongst the white people, but separated as far as possible; they have their own churches and schools, and travel on the railways in coaches specially reserved for them.

When we think of the importance of Australia and New Zealand, it is difficult to believe that these lands were almost unknown to Europeans until the end of the 18th century. Dutch seamen had previously explored part of the coast of Australia and found an uninviting land. The English explorer Dampier, who landed on the north-west coast, described the interior as the most barren spot on earth.

In 1770, however, Captain Cook, who had already claimed possession of New Zealand in the name of George III, proceeded to explore the eastern shores of Australia; he found a rich and fruitful country.

Eighteen years later, the first British settlement was

made at the point where Sydney now stands, and the colony of New South Wales was proclaimed. During the first half of the 19th century settlements were made in Victoria, Tasmania, South Australia, Western Australia and Queensland, as well as in the New Zealand islands; in the early stages settlement was greatly encouraged by discoveries of gold. The Australian colonies have developed into states, and with Tasmania, they constitute the Commonwealth of Australia. New Zealand is a separate Dominion.

Australian aborigines, commonly called "blackfellows" though they do not belong to the negro family, still exist in a nomadic state in the interior of the continent. Their number is dwindling. The Maoris of New Zealand are a more stalwart people. Many have nomadic habits, but in South Island they live generally in European fashion. About ten thousand Maori children are in regular attendance at Day Schools. The Maoris have four members of parliament.

Another region that has been settled in recent times is Siberia. This country has always been occupied by nomads, but the area over which they can roam has been somewhat reduced by Russian immigrants, who farm the rich land in the South. At one time the white population of Siberia consisted chiefly of exiles and convicts, but the building of the trans-continental railway and the offer of cheap land, led to a great influx of "willing" colonists. The tide of emigration from Russia to Siberia reached a very high level at the time of the revolution (1917).

Thus there is a narrow belt of white population extending through Asia to the Pacific shores. Portions of the yellow race still occupy the vast plains (tundras) that border the Arctic Ocean—not in Asia only, but also in Europe and America. Amongst the best-known groups are the Eskimos (North America), the Lapps (Europe), the Samoyedes and the Yakuts (Siberia); all of them live a nomadic or semi-nomadic life.

EXERCISES

1. Explain the terms "Stone Age," "Bronze Age" and "Iron Age." In what age do we live?

2. Give reasons why civilisation made rapid progress in the Mediterranean region, in ancient times.

3. Write short notes on "Red Indians," "Maoris" and "Blackfellows."

4. With the help of your atlas, name the settlements and trading stations indicated by the arrows in the map on page 143.

XIII. FOODSTUFFS AND RAW MATERIALS

1. AGRICULTURAL FOODSTUFFS

"As for the earth, out of it cometh bread," says the Book of Job, reminding us that the surface of the earth yields everything required to sustain human life—fruit, grain and vegetables, and herbage for the animals which provide flesh food for man.

As we have already noticed (chap. XI), natural vegetation and cultivated crops are controlled by climate, and therefore to some extent by latitude. Thus it has been found possible to mark on a map of Europe the northern "limit" of wheat, that is, the line beyond which wheat cannot be grown successfully. Such lines have also been drawn for the olive, the vine

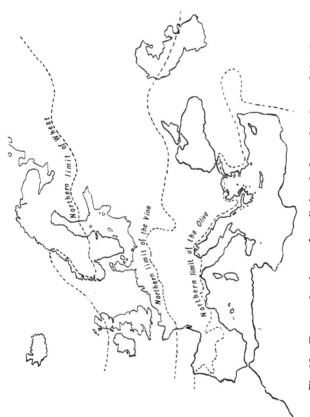

Fig. 32. Europe, showing northern limits of wheat, the vine, and the olive. There is also an altitude limit; the higher parts of the Alps, Pyrenees, Caucasus, and other mountain systems have an Alpine or Arctic flora.

and other plants. There are of course corresponding "limits" with respect to altitude.

First in importance amongst the world's food crops are wheat and rice, each of which forms the staple food of about one-third of the population of the world.

Wheat is the chief food in the greater part of Europe, in the United States and in the British Empire. The plant requires a moist spring and a warm dry summer. It therefore grows well in the interior of North America, in the south of Russia (Ukraine), Mediterranean lands of both Europe and Africa, India, Australia and Argentina. Wheat is ripening in one land or another in almost every month of the year.

In Britain, wheat is grown chiefly in the eastern counties, where the rainfall is less than 30 inches (see page 5). But the home supplies are sufficient for but a quarter of the population. Much more might be grown, but English farmers generally prefer to put their land under grass, and produce meat, milk, butter and cheese. They find it difficult to compete with the grain-growers of Canada and the United States, who have large level tracts of land on which labour-saving machinery can be used with advantage.

Oats and barley, cereals of a hardy type, are generally grown in wheat-producing countries. Rye is grown largely on poor land in central Europe. Maize, the principal food of the people of Mexico, requires a warm and rather moist climate. It is grown in America, south of the wheat belt, and in the States it is used mostly for feeding the animals that go to the meat factories of Chicago. Vast quantities are grown on the plains of south-eastern Europe.

Rice is the chief food in the east and south-east of

Asia, in the valleys of India, and in parts of Africa and South America. The variety most commonly grown requires plenty of warmth and moisture; it is usually grown on low-lying land which can be flooded easily. Though cultivated to some extent in northern Italy and the United States, rice thrives best in lands that have a hot wet summer. We may sum up by saying

Labour-saving Machinery, on a Canadian Grain-land.

that rice is a monsoon crop. European supplies come chiefly from Burma. India, China and Japan consume all the rice they grow.

The potato deserves special mention. Introduced into Europe from the Andes region, it was at first regarded with but little favour. Now, its valuable qualities are recognised, and it is grown in nearly every country in the temperate zones.

Many and varied are the foods consumed by the rest

of the world's peoples. Millet is found in the homes of the Egyptians and the inhabitants of the Indian plateau. Sago, made from the pith of the sago-palm, is used by many East Indian people, bread-fruit and coconut by the dwellers in the South Sea islands. The banana and plantain have also a place in the diet of the Pacific islanders, and these fruits are valuable foods in the tropical parts of Africa and South America and especially in the West Indies. Manioc is a plant whose tubers provide sustenance for the half-savage inhabitants of the Amazon region—after its poisonous juice has been extracted. It is also the source of tapioca.

The sugar-cane, tea, coffee, cacao (cocoa) and the fruits grown in various regions have been mentioned in chapter XI (pages 123 to 127). An additional point of some interest is that, whereas Russians and English-speaking people in all parts of the world show a decided preference for tea, the inhabitants of western Europe generally use large quantities of coffee but very little tea. We may also note that Spain is the one European country that prefers cocoa as a beverage, though Switzerland, with its great chocolate industry, has a greater average consumption of cocoa.

2. PASTORAL FOODSTUFFS

Man's "staff of life" is derived from the plant world, but most people consider a certain amount of flesh food desirable, if not absolutely necessary. Meat is obtained chiefly from domesticated animals, though in some countries, wild or semi-wild creatures, such as deer, grouse, pheasants and others, make considerable contributions to man's larder. The chief domesticated animals are cattle, sheep, pigs, goats, and in the far north, reindeer, caribou and musk-oxen.

Animals are reared for food in almost all countries. Most British farmers work their land by the method called "mixed farming"; that is, they combine agriculture with pastoral work. Where the land varies greatly in character this is an ideal method. Sheep and some species of cattle will thrive on the poor herbage of rock-strewn fells, which are useless for crop-raising, whilst milk cows can be fed and crops can be grown on the richer land of the valleys and plains.

There are in the world, however, many large tracts of land which, by reason of long periods of drought and absence of rivers, are unsuitable for agriculture. Such are the steppes of Central Asia, the plateaux of the Middle East, the Savannas of Central Africa, and the scrub-lands that border the great deserts. In these regions pastoral work is the rule. The inhabitants possess sheep, goats, cattle, and in some cases camels. The needs of their animals compel them to lead a nomadic life, as did the patriarchs in bible history. They move from one pasture-land to another, carrying with them their tents and household goods; they live largely upon the products of their flocks and herds.

Even civilised countries contain areas somewhat similar to those described in the last paragraph. As examples we may mention the veld of South Africa, the Canterbury Plains of New Zealand, a vast grassland west of the Australian mountains, the pampas of Argentina, and the home of that famous character, the cow-boy—the Great Plains of North America. Portions of these have been "reclaimed" by means of costly irrigation works; but large areas are still devoted entirely to pastoral work.

The numbers of animals fed in these regions are truly enormous. Australia and Argentina for instance have 113 million and 50 million sheep respectively; Argentina has 31 million cattle and Australia 11 million. The number of sheep in New Zealand is smaller (30 million), but considering its area, New Zealand is the greatest sheep-rearing country in the world. Each of these three countries has a small population; the flocks and herds they possess are altogether out of proportion to the needs of the people. The same may be said of the American plains, and in a smaller degree of South Africa. It should be remembered that in the latter country oxen are in great demand for drawing wagons.

Australia, New Zealand, Argentina and North America have therefore become meat providers for other lands, and especially for England, where more people are engaged in manufactures than in food production. Meat exported from Australia, New Zealand and Argentina is frozen or "chilled" and conveyed in cold storage on vessels specially fitted for the trade; but much meat is sent from America, and some from Argentina, packed in airtight tins.

Other animal foods are fish, hams and bacon, milk, butter and cheese, the first of which has been noticed on page 136. Dairy produce and bacon are products of temperate regions, and it is an interesting fact that farmers engaged in dairy-work frequently take up pig-rearing as a companion industry. Thus we receive butter and bacon from Denmark and Ireland, bacon and cheese from Canada. Condensed milk, enclosed in airtight tins, is exported from Switzerland, Ireland and

Sweden. Cold storage has made it possible for butter to be sent to English markets from such distant lands as Australia, New Zealand, Canada and Siberia.

3. RAW MATERIALS

We have already mentioned the industrial value of coal and other minerals found in sedimentary rocks. But many industries cannot be carried on with coal and iron only; all parts of the world, and both animal kingdom and plant kingdom, are called upon to supply raw materials for the factories of Britain and other industrial countries. Some of the more important of these are mentioned below.

From the cold northern forests come pelts of the black fox, sable, beaver, stone-marten and others, collected by Indian trappers for the Hudson Bay Company, and by Siberian nomads for the markets of Russia and Germany.

More important substances come from temperate lands. Thus we have wool and skins from the sheep-rearing lands, and wool or hair from the alpaca and vicuna of the lofty Andes, and the Angora goat of Asia Minor.

The plant world provides some most useful fibres. Flax, the raw material for the linen trade, is grown in Russia and Belgium, and jute, an Indian product, is used for coarser fabrics such as gunny bags which are used for packing purposes. Hemp, a strong fibre for rope-making, is obtained from Russia and Italy. The East Indies produces two serious rivals to hemp—Manila "hemp," and China grass or ramie. The latter has two good qualities, silky appearance and great strength, which make it suitable for the manufacture of such different things as ropes and table linen.

Most important of all plant fibres is cotton. For many years the United States, India and Egypt were the chief cotton-producing lands. Now there are plantations in Queensland, and in Nigeria, the Sudan and other British possessions in Africa.

West Africa has been described as the land of rubber, oil, and ivory. The oils are palm-oil and coconut oil, largely used in the manufacture of soap. A commodity of equal value is olive-oil, produced in all Mediterranean lands, where it is of importance as a food; it has a rival in cotton-seed oil. The valuable timbers yielded by the world's forests are described in chapter XI.

EXERCISES

1. What is meant by "staple food"? What is the staple food of the Japanese, the Hindus, the Eskimos, the Mexicans, and the Bedouin Arabs?

2. Name countries that produce a surplus of (*a*) wheat, (*b*) rice, (*c*) meat, (*d*) fruit.

3. Make out lists of foods and beverages you take regularly, which come from tropical lands and from temperate lands.

4. On an outline map of the world mark the wheat-routes, meat-routes, cotton-routes and tea-routes—that is the routes by which the commodities named come to Britain.

XIV. TRADE AND TRANSPORT

1. OVER-SEAS TRADE

The needs of human beings are now so many and so varied that few regions can provide all that is required by their inhabitants. One area produces a surplus of foodstuffs; another more manufactured articles than its population can use; but each is dependent upon the other.

In the densely populated industrial parts of England, for example, so much attention is paid to manufactures, and so much land is devoted to the working of minerals, that the home-grown food is far from being sufficient, and great quantities are brought from abroad.

Our own land will not even produce the raw materials used in manufactures. Neither cotton nor rubber can be grown under English climatic conditions; wool is not now produced by British sheep in quantity sufficient to satisfy the demands of our factories; our forests supply neither the amount nor the variety of timber which is needed in various industries.

It is clear then that England depends for her existence on trade with other lands. The commodities named are brought from the wheat-lands of America and India; from the cotton-fields of the United States, India, and Egypt; from the rubber plantations of the Amazon, the Congo and the East Indies; from the forests of America and the Baltic countries; from the sheep farms of Australia, New Zealand and Argentina.

England in return sends out coal and all kinds of manufactured goods. She supplies machinery for use in the Canadian wheat-lands; rails and locomotives for the carriage of goods in Argentina and elsewhere. She sends out cotton fabrics to the agricultural peoples of India and Egypt; and ready-made clothing for the colonists in Australia and New Zealand.

The carriage of goods across the seas employs a great number of steam and sailing vessels. Between important commercial lands there is a regular service of merchant vessels, traversing certain recognised routes called **ocean-lanes.**

The vessels owned by one firm constitute a **line.**

Amongst famous British lines are the Cunard-White

The *Queen Mary* (*Associated Press photo*)

Star, P. and O. (Peninsular and Oriental), R.M.S.P. (Royal Mail Steam Packet Company), Elder Dempster, Blue Funnel, and Union Castle.

The Cunard-White Star steamship *Queen Mary* (80,773 tons) is the largest British vessel afloat. Only a few months after her maiden trip to New York, she recaptured for Britain the "blue riband" of the Atlantic, with an average speed of 30·63 knots, in 1936. She burns 1200 tons of oil fuel per day. Her rival, the

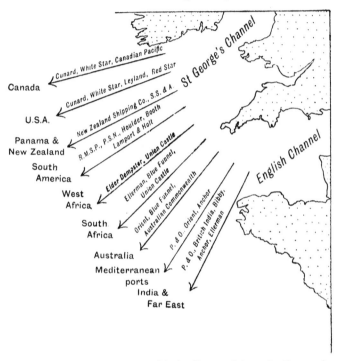

Fig. 33. Some of the great British shipping lines, and the routes they work.

Normandie (82,779 tons), is a French ship, built at St Nazaire, at the mouth of the Loire.

The P. and O. liners use the Suez Canal. They sail from Tilbury, about 20 miles down the Thames from London Bridge.

The Canadian Pacific Railway has its own fleet of steamers on both the Atlantic and the Pacific.

Many liners carry both passengers and cargo. Some are devoted entirely to trade, and, if engaged in conveyance of oil, or frozen meat, are of special construction. There are many other vessels, called **tramps**, which do not run between a certain pair of ports. They go anywhere and carry almost anything, except such special cargoes as oil. They take an important part in the carriage of coal from British ports, and bring back whatever can be picked up. The chief British lines and the routes they work are named in the diagram.

Commercial lands must have good harbours. As the estuary of a river enables a ship to penetrate some distance into the country, with the assistance of the tide, it is valuable for commerce. A port is built near the head of the tidal waterway and others grow up on both banks of the lower river. The Tyne has six towns and the Mersey an equal number.

Railway wagons are brought alongside the vessels. Then goods are transferred direct from ship to truck.

So quickly is the work of unloading carried out that the cargo of a vessel reaching port in the evening is frequently distributed in the chief towns of the country next morning.

This means, of course, that a seaport must have very good railway connections. The success of a port depends not only on its equipment for handling cargo, but to a great extent also on the means of communication inland. Many railway companies are indeed the owners of docks. Ports depend upon railways for their existence, but the latter derive much benefit from connection with a port. The London and North Eastern Railway owns most of the busy docks on the Humber, Tees and

A N.E. Railway dock scene, illustrating rapid transfer of cargo. Timber is lifted direct from ship to railway wagon.

Tyne, and some of those on the Forth; the London Midland and Scottish has docks at Fleetwood, Heysham, Barrow-in-Furness, and Grangemouth; the Great Western owns most of the docks in South Wales, and the Southern Railway the great liner port of Southampton.

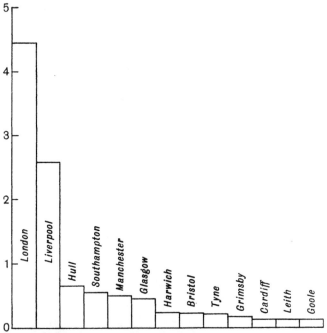

Fig. 34. Diagram showing the relative importance of the leading British seaports, judged by the *value* of their import and export trade in 1934.

Each unit on the vertical line represents £100,000,000.

You will learn all about the work of our ports when you study the geography of Britain; but important features in connection with one or two may be noticed now.

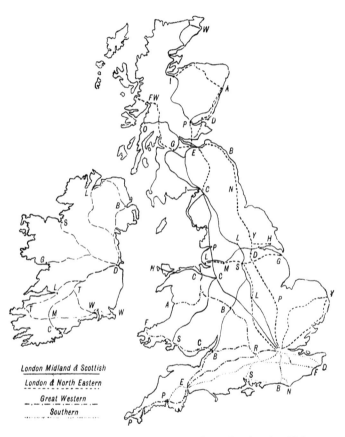

Fig. 35.   Railway map of the British Isles, showing the chief
branches of the four great railways of Britain.

(Copy this map on a larger outline and enter the lines in different
colours, say red, green, blue, black.   Name the towns in full.)

London is supreme as a port. In and around the city there are nearly ten million people, demanding the products of other lands. London supplies not her immediate neighbourhood only, but all parts of the country, with which it is connected by four great railway systems. A walk along the quays and through the warehouses of the Port of London would afford an excellent oppor-

Ivory Floor, London Docks.

tunity to learn the products of all parts of the earth's surface.

There is grain from Canada, Argentina, India and Russia; wool from New Zealand, Australia, and the Argentine; spices from the East and West Indies; countless chests of tea from India, Ceylon and China; hogsheads of tobacco from America and the West Indies; meat from New Zealand and Argentina; timber, oils, rubber, hides, ivory, feathers—there is everything you could mention, being prepared for distribution, or re-export. London's imports are worth three times her exports.

Liverpool as a port has suffered through the depression in the cotton industry. Its trade is now only a little more than half that of the port of London, and exports balance imports in value. It serves four industrial

Wool Floor, London Docks.

regions—the Lancashire cotton area, the Yorkshire woollen and engineering towns, the Staffordshire Potteries and the engineering and hardware area of the Midlands. Liverpool, well connected by rail and canal with all of them, is the chief inlet and outlet for the first region, and a secondary port for the other three.

It must not be supposed that cotton goods are exported only through Liverpool. The port selected

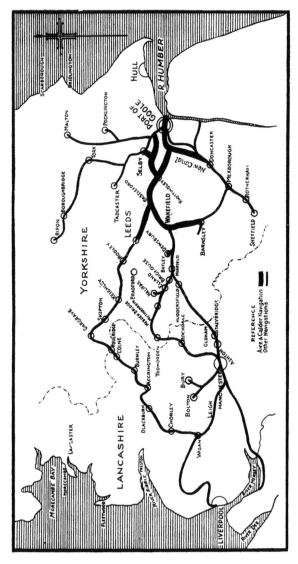

Fig. 36. Map of the 700 miles water-transport system of northern England, including the Manchester Ship Canal, Leeds and Liverpool Canal, Aire and Calder Navigation, and some smaller canals. Many towns and villages not marked on the map are connected with the waterway by motor lorries and other road vehicles.

depends upon the destination of the goods; the same may be said of all other articles.

The Humber ports, Hull, Grimsby and Goole, command British trade with the Baltic countries and Northern Asia; they import enormous quantities of grain, dairy produce, timber, pit props and oil-seeds. Their chief exports are what one would expect, considering the district that lies behind them—machinery, cotton and woollen goods and, from Hull, coal.

Hull now ranks third among British ports. The Aire

Hull Dock Scene.

and Calder Navigation scheme, together with the Leeds and Liverpool canal and others, forms a waterway from sea to sea, through two coalfields and the textile and engineering regions of Yorkshire and Lancashire. Five out of six of our largest fishing ports are on the east coast of Britain—Hull and Grimsby, Yarmouth and Lowestoft, and Aberdeen. Fleetwood is on the Lancashire coast. Specially-built vessels carry fish quickly from the **trawlers** into port, and distribution inland is carried out by means of special fish-trains to the big centres of population.

The ports of the North East Coast import builders' timber and pit props. Shipbuilding is important in each of the three estuaries (Tyne, Wear, Tees). In normal times the Tyne ranks next to the Clyde as a shipbuilding river and second only to South Wales as a coal-exporting outlet.

Southampton is chiefly important as a great passenger port within easy reach of London. It has the advantage of double tides. Large quantities of foodstuffs (mainly meat) are landed.

2. Some Inland Distribution Centres

The distribution inland of foreign produce landed at our ports is carried out by waterways, railways and roads, and naturally there will be centres in the interior for detailed distribution. A town which is situated where several routes meet will have the best possible chance of becoming a thriving place. In fact it is at such points that busy towns arise; they develop as the volume of trade increases.

Manchester is of course a great distributing centre for the thickly peopled cotton-manufacturing county. It possesses the immense advantage of a connection with the sea by means of the Ship Canal, a waterway 28 feet deep, and therefore navigable by the lesser liners. It now ranks fifth among British ports (see fig. 34).

The centre of the city is crowded with warehouses and offices. The removal of factories to the outskirts of the city and to the neighbouring towns is a good indication of the change which has taken place in the activities of Manchester during the last thirty years.

Leeds, the chief distributing centre in Yorkshire,

Hartlepool Timber Store. (Pit props for northern coalfields.)

has communication by rail, river and canal with ports on the east, and on the west coasts.

The river Aire is navigable, and links the city with the Humber. The Leeds and Liverpool canal passing through a break in the Pennines called the **Aire Gap** connects west Yorkshire with the Mersey, and is greatly used. A canal wharf scene in a large town is not unlike a dock, except for the different aspect of the vessels. Many barges are driven by steam, and carry cargoes of

Steam tug towing a load of 800 tons of coal, on the Aire and Calder Navigation System. The coal is conveyed in a train of steel boxes, in front of which is a "headpiece," shaped like the prow of a boat.

perishable nature such as grain. Leeds is fortunate in the possession of means of communication through the Pennines. Indeed if there had been no gap, there would possibly have been no city. For, examining the map, you will notice other Yorkshire dales, the upper ends of which pass into high land and bleak moors. Wharfedale, Nidderdale, Wensleydale and Swaledale are their names. They are quite famous as holiday-grounds, for they are such peaceful valleys as are appreciated by an industrial population. As in the case of Airedale, there is a town at the entrance to each, for the people in the dales must receive supplies from the outer world, and these **valley-mouth** towns serve as market towns for

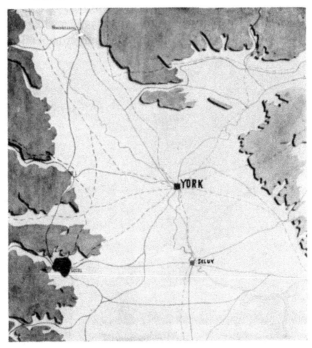

Fig. 37. Photograph of Relief-map of the Vale of York, showing railways and roads (dotted) which radiate from the city. The crooked line is the river Ouse. The shaded portion represents land having altitude of over 300 ft.

them. But these towns, Otley, Wetherby, Harrogate, Ripon, Richmond, away from the coalfield, are, as the railway traffic shows, sub-centres to Leeds.

York occupies a commanding position on the east

coast route from London to Scotland. Railways and roads radiate from the city in every direction. The Great North Road does not pass through York, but through Boroughbridge. The York route carries more traffic, however.

Perhaps York might be described as **a sorting-town**. Goods which reach the city by the numerous railways

Aerial view of part of the Port of Goole, showing locks (500 feet long) at entrance, warehouses, railway tracks on the wharves, and river Ouse in the background. The four tall black structures beside the water are coal hoists.

are sorted and sent forward without ever going into the city proper. Since so many roads lead to York, the huge railway station is an important sorting-place for passengers also. No less important as railway centres are Edinburgh, Carlisle and Crewe; others may be found in the map on page 161.

Now though the industrial regions support the greater part of the population of Britain, they occupy only a minor portion of the area of our land. The rest of the country is devoted in the main to agriculture— including both cultivation of the soil and rearing of cattle, horses and sheep.

Such regions are not so much dependent upon the products of other lands as manufacturing districts are,

East Coast Express. (On the L.N.E. section.)

and in the past, obtaining food from their crops and raw material for the manufacture of clothing from their flocks and herds, were entirely self-supporting.

The towns are distributing centres, mainly for home products. They are market-towns, sleepy enough as a rule but now wakened up by motor traffic and bustling with life and activity on market-days, when people from the surrounding country cart in their produce for disposal.

Appleby in Westmorland, Malton and Pickering,

one on each side of the Vale of Pickering, are typical
market-towns in the North; but it is in the part of
England which lies on the south-eastern side of the
oolitic ridge that the agricultural population chiefly
lives and market-towns are most typical.

Between this ridge and the chalk hills, the clay vale
is given up to mixed farming and poultry. The chief

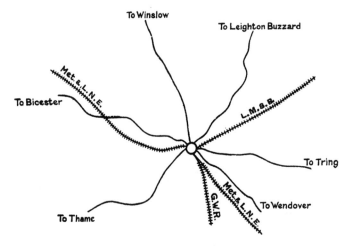

Fig. 38.　Roads and Railways from Aylesbury to the
surrounding agricultural area.

towns are Bedford, Aylesbury, Leighton Buzzard and
Oxford. Most of them developed centuries ago at points
which were convenient for the exchange of goods.

Eastwards of the chalk hills there lies another
agricultural area—the chief wheat-growing district in
England. Norwich and Ipswich, in addition to being
important market-towns, are engaged in the manufacture of agricultural implements.

These and other areas suffered greatly during the industrial development of the last 150 years. There are indications at present, however, of a determination to secure a better position in the commercial world, and this is being helped by modern motor traffic.

The dairy produce of Devonshire and Somerset has gained a place in the markets of the great manufacturing towns; and though the foreigner will probably never lose his hold on this branch of British trade, there is every chance for our own people to obtain a greater share.

EXERCISES

1. Make diagrams to show the lines of communication inland from London, Liverpool, Glasgow and Southampton.

2. On an outline map of the North Sea, or Europe, mark the positions of the chief British ports and those on the continent with which they trade.

3. With the aid of a newspaper make a list of steamship "lines" connecting the ports mentioned in Exercise 1 with distant ports.

4. With the help of a railway guide, and the map on page 161, give two routes by which a person may travel from London to Glasgow. Find the time occupied, and the names of towns where a stop is made.

5. Large quantities of wool are landed at Liverpool, London and the Humber ports. Name the countries from which the wool is brought, the towns for which it is intended, and the routes by which it is conveyed from the ports.

6. What purpose is served by lighthouses, lightships, beacons and buoys?

7. Select the chief town in your own district, and show in a diagram the roads and railways which link it to neighbouring towns and villages.

XV. SOME GREAT WORLD-ROUTES

We live in days of great enterprises.   In all parts
of the world attempts are being made to shorten the
journey between lands which produce and those which
consume.

In spite of obstacles to railway construction offered

Rail-laying, on the Canadian National Railway.

by great systems of mountains, America is crossed by
eight railway routes.

They link Atlantic and Pacific ports which are over
3000 miles apart.

Connected by steamships, on the one hand with
Europe and on the other with the Far East, the Canadian
Pacific and Canadian National railways form the middle
portion of a 12,000 miles route.

The Union Pacific is the corresponding link in the United States route; west of Denver the line rises at one point to 11,000 ft. above sea-level.

In Africa, the Cape to Cairo railway scheme is in progress. "This line," said the late Cecil Rhodes, "will be the backbone and spinal cord to direct, consolidate and give life to the numerous systems of side railways, which will connect the vast central road with the seas on either hand."

In Asia there are two trans-continental railways, one of which, the Baghdad line, is not yet completed. In a few years it will be possible to travel across the Strait of Dover, then by the Orient express to Constantinople, through Asia Minor to the region known as the Middle East. Mesopotamia forms a portion of this region. Irrigation works are expected to make the land into an important wheat-growing area. Even now it is the chief date-growing region in the world. The railway will greatly help to revive a country which was once prosperous.

The trans-Siberian railway provides land communication between the west of Europe and the Far East. It has placed the important cities of Tokio and Shanghai within 14 days' journey of London.

It is becoming more and more important as a trade-route, and carries wheat, dairy produce, tea and other agricultural products westwards. A traveller has recently given an interesting account of the journey.

"One enters a luxurious train de luxe at Moscow of the ordinary *wagon-lits* type, the coaches being divided into a series of two-berth cabins. A week later one exchanges it for another equally luxurious at Irkutsk. Three days later a change of gauge at Chang Chun necessitates another new train, which, after a further change at Mukden on to the Pekin-Mukden line, deposits one finally at Pekin. Passengers to Japan go straight through from Moscow to Vladivostock without any change at all."

Describing the journey through Siberia, she continues, "Hour after hour the train rolls through an interminable succession of cornfields, varied by clover, potatoes and cabbages. Except in the neighbourhood of Lake Baikal there is nothing remarkable along the route in the way of scenery, save the claim which lies in open spaces and a wide sky-line. In the course of the twelve-days' journey some wooded and undulating country is traversed, but in the main steppe yields place to steppe, plain to plain, from Russia through Manchuria.....From the vast treeless plains of Manchuria one glides insensibly into China without effort of any kind. The log cabins of Siberia give way to the mud houses with reed-thatched roofs; little by little the blue-gowned Chinaman with his straw hat becomes a familiar object in the fields. Walled villages become common, and between Chang Chun and Mukden, a district infested by brigands, isolated and farm houses are protected by walls with loop-holes for firing purposes. But the great plain still persists, though we have now passed into golden fields of kaoling—the greater millet, and Soya beans." (Violet Markham in the *Westminster Gazette*, Feb. 1914.)

A comparatively short trans-continental route is the railway that links the South American ports, Buenos Aires and Valparaiso. Trains do not run through from coast to coast, because there is a change of gauge in the mountain region.

Australia also possesses a trans-continental railway

route. The final link was a line between Port Augusta and Kalgoorlie, completed in 1917. It is now possible to travel by train from Perth to all the other Australian capitals; but there are several changes of gauge on the route. The through journey from Perth to Brisbane is one of 3372 miles. It takes six days!

The Suez Canal, opened in 1869, is 100 miles in length from Port Said to Suez. Previously, the connection between the Mediterranean and Indian Ocean liners had been made across the isthmus which linked Africa to Asia, by camels. Sometimes several thousand camels would be required to transport the merchandise of a single vessel. The opening of the canal made a great change in the traffic to the Far East. There was a great reduction in cost, as well as a saving of time. The voyage to Australia and New Zealand was also shortened by over a thousand miles, though, as you will see from shipping advertisements, many liners still follow the **Cape route.** Canal dues are heavy. Vessels of more than 30,000 tons are as a matter of fact excluded from the Suez Canal because the water is not deep enough.

An even greater engineering work is the Panama Canal, opened in 1914.

You must study the map of the world carefully, and remember that lands on the western side of North and South America are wonderfully rich in commercial products, to know what this canal means to the trade centres of Europe. The voyage from England to New Zealand is only shortened by about three days, but the journey to some of the South Sea islands, has been reduced by a fortnight.

Vancouver, San Francisco, Valparaiso and other ports on the Pacific shores of America are also "brought

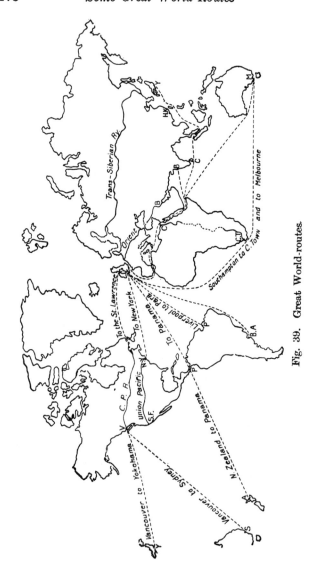

Fig. 39.   Great World-routes.

nearer" London. The voyage to Vancouver can now be made in three weeks less time than formerly. The canal therefore provides for British Columbia a much wanted additional means of communication with Atlantic ports. South American states, such as Chile and Peru, are in a better position for dealing with important markets.

Considering that the distance across the isthmus of Panama is not more than 50 miles, you may be surprised that the canal was not cut long ago. In justice to former generations it must be stated that the work was commenced—about 50 years ago. But yellow fever carried off great numbers of workmen, and the scheme was abandoned.

In 1902 the United States determined to carry out the work. She began by buying the canal zone and making it healthy by draining the swamps. The canal is 85 ft. above sea level and is entered by locks.

More remarkable than all these enterprises is **the conquest of the air.** Only as recently as the year 1903 did man really learn to fly. That year an American, Orville Wright, flew nearly 300 yards in just under a minute. He flew 20 miles in 1906. In 1909 M. Bleriot flew across the Dover Channel from France. From these early beginnings and especially since 1919 "flying" has developed as rapidly as railways did after George Stephenson ran his first train in 1825. The twentieth century is indeed a New Age. You can fly from London to Paris in about an hour and a half, with three services a day each way. There are now air-routes between all the great capitals and to the remotest cities of the British Empire. A route of first importance follows the Mediterranean-Baghdad way to India, Colombo, Singapore, Port Darwin and the Australian capitals.

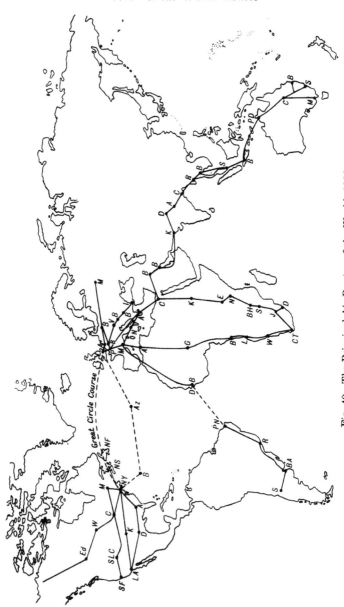

Fig. 40. The Principal Air Routes of the World, 1936.

[Copy this map on to a larger outline and fill in the names of towns.]

Karachi is reached from London in six days, flying in the daytime only, Colombo in eight, Singapore in ten and Sydney in fifteen days. Even this will quickly be improved upon.

Three main airways cross Africa from north to south. The one most used is mainly British and might well be called the "Cape-to-Cairo route by air". A probable route (mainly French) will run from Algiers or Oran to the Cape by way of the Sahara desert and Nigeria. It follows the west coast of Central and South Africa. A third route makes for Cape Verde (Dakar, in French Senegal or Bathurst in British Gambia) and crosses the narrowest part of the Atlantic to Port Natal, in Brazil. Thence you can fly on to Rio, Buenos Aires and Santiago reaching the latter in little over a week.

The commercial use of the aeroplane in the U.S.A. is greater than that of all the rest of the world put together. Aviators will not be content until regular services are established between Western Europe and North America. Many experimental flights have been made in the last few years and it is expected that the year 1937 will see regular passenger, mail and freight services working to schedule. The great circle route from Croydon to New York passes St Johns (N.F.) and Halifax (N.S.). An alternative route is *via* the Azores and Bermuda. The difficulty of these long non-stop flights across an ocean is the heavy load of petrol the machine must carry, which means they can take much less freight than if they could halt for refuelling every 500 miles or so. This is arranged for on the land-routes. Regular "air-liners" cruise at from 100 to 150 miles an hour, but speeds of 200 miles an hour will soon be attained. Journeys of 1000 miles a day are quite usual. As many as 50 passengers and a ton or two of mails and cargo can be carried. To-day you can buy a "Bradshaw" of the air! It is called the International Air Guide.

For haste and for mails the aeroplane is valuable; but for general use and heavy freights, ocean vessels will hold their own. The *Queen Mary* can carry 2140 passengers and a crew of 1100! On the other hand, thirty knots is good going on the sea.

Pioneer aviators, both men and women, out to break records and open up new routes, fly non-stop at excessively high speeds and under exhausting conditions. Particulars of their wonderful flights are given every year in Whitaker's Almanack. For many years to come new and safer and ever faster machines will be built and the conquest of the air will go on until all the principal cities of the world are linked together in one great network, as they are already by rail-roads and sea-routes.

Study carefully Fig. 40; add to it new lines as they begin to operate. As the network grows you will see how closely it resembles the existing network of trade routes by land and sea. This is because they serve the same cities and populous regions.

In the air mountains and deserts cease to be barriers. The chief obstacles, apart from fogs, are political. Permission has to be obtained to fly over foreign countries. Will the day ever come when the air is as free as the sea? I wonder. Perhaps you will live to see it.

EXERCISES

1. On an outline map of North America mark the courses of the Canadian Pacific, Canadian National, and Union Pacific railways. Insert the chief towns and rivers.

2. Use the scale of miles printed on your atlas map, and find roughly the distance from Halifax to Vancouver; and assuming the average rate of a train to be 30 miles per hour, find how long it would take to cross the continent.

3. On your map of Africa trace the route of the Cape to Cairo line (not yet completed) through the following: Cape Town, Kimberley, Mafeking, Buluwayo, Elizabethville, Congolo, Stanleyville, Gondokoro, Khartum, Berber, Wady Halfa, Assuan, Cairo.

4. Trace the course of a vessel from London to Bombay. Name important call-places en route.

5. With the help of a newspaper containing shipping advertisements, make out a list of British steamship lines most affected by the opening of the Panama Canal.

GENERAL INDEX

INDEX OF PLACE-NAMES

For EU product safety concerns, contact us at Calle de José Abascal, 56–1°,
28003 Madrid, Spain or eugpsr@cambridge.org.